MY
LIFE
AS AN
EXPLORER

EYEWITNESS ACCOUNTS

MY LIFE AS AN EXPLORER

ROALD AMUNDSEN

INTRODUCTION BY CAMPBELL McCUTCHEON

AMBERLEY

First published 2014

Amberley Publishing
The Hill, Stroud
Gloucestershire, GL5 4EP

www.amberley-books.com

British Library Cataloguing in Publication Data.
A catalogue record for this book is available from the British Library.

ISBN 978 1 4456 3580 4

Typeset in 10pt on 12pt Sabon.
Typesetting and Origination by Amberley Publishing.
Printed in the UK.

CONTENTS

The *Gjoa*, 72 feet long and 11 feet wide and of shallow draft, used by Amundsen in his discovery of the Northwest Passage and now on view at the Golden Gate Park in San Francisco.

Introduction

Born on 16 July 1872 in Borge, Norway, Roald Amundsen was destined to become an explorer. From his earliest days he worked with a phenomenal determination towards this goal. It was his reading of the works of Sir John Franklin, the intrepid explorer of the North West Passage, that set his life on a course that made him the first man to reach the South Pole, the first to reach the North Pole by dirigible, and the first man to conquer the North West Passage – a feat Franklin had died trying to achieve.

The life of an explorer is a hard one, and one that requires much time spent gathering the necessary funds to achieve one's goals. Amundsen knew this only too well, taking his *Gjoa* from Norway in the dead of night on 16 June 1903 on a three-year voyage to the frozen wastes of the Arctic to trace the route of the North West Passage. Having left his brother to deal with his creditors, Amundsen and his friends set sail for Greenland. For three years they sailed in summer and lay trapped in winter quarters in the frozen ice before breaking through from the Arctic Ocean into the Pacific.

The journey was not his first into the frozen wastes, but it was the first that Amundsen had organized. His journey to the Antarctic as First Mate aboard the Belgian polar vessel *Belgica* had shown him the value of organization and planning, or rather the disastrous problems created by a lack of planning and organization. Meticulous preparation was to be a feature of each and every journey Amundsen would undertake. In 1910 he set sail in Nansen's old ship, the *Fram*, for Madeira, where he cabled Robert Falcon Scott, in Australia at the time, to tell him of his plans to conquer the South Pole.

Scott had a two-month advantage over Amundsen for the quest, but his planning was not as good. Amundsen took dogs with him, both as transport and as food, while Scott used new-fangled motor sleds and Shetland ponies. Amundsen's plans included eating the dogs as they weakened, and his route to the Pole was shorter and easier. He reached the Pole two weeks before Scott; the rest is history. Amundsen brought all of his men back alive, while Scott, Oates, Bowers, Evans and Wilson died on their failed attempt.

During the First World War Amundsen invested in shipping, amassing a small fortune which he used to further his polar exploration. He had seen the virtues of aircraft before the war, purchasing a Farman in 1914. This aircraft was never used, being donated to the fledgling Norwegian air force instead. After the war ended, Amundsen equipped himself with a new Junkers, but problems with the undercarriage made it unsuitable for polar work. A Curtis was used next, followed by two Dornier seaplanes in 1925 for an expedition from Spitzbergen over the polar icecap. One of the seaplanes broke down as it landed, and both seaplanes became trapped in the ice. For three weeks Amundsen and his crews made efforts to release the aircraft. The world feared that he, his adventurer financier Lincoln Ellsworth and the crews had died, but by cutting a runway through the ice and making a very risky take-off, the adventurers escaped back to Spitzbergen after a flight to 88 degrees north.

The following year Amundsen and Ellsworth purchased the *N-1*, an Italian airship, renamed it *Norge*, and set out for Spitzbergen with the Italian Nobile as pilot. Despite numerous setbacks, a successful flight was made over the polar icecap from Kings Bay, Spitzbergen, to Teller, near Nome, Alaska. After seventy-two hours' flying, the *Norge* had succeeded in flying from continent to continent over the polar ice. Despite its success, the flight was not without its problems; but these were of a personal nature. The conflict that existed between the Italian pilot Nobile and the commander of the expedition, Amundsen, runs through the chapters relating to this historic flight.

Amundsen's life was one of adventure, and it was to be ended in mysterious circumstances somewhere in the polar regions. Always prepared, always organized, with plans for every eventuality, Amundsen's demise is a mystery. Retired from exploration, he set off from Tromso in June 1928 in search of Nobile and the crew of the airship *Italia*, which had crashed on the return from the North Pole. Amundsen and his five companions, in a Latham 47 floatplane, simply disappeared, the only trace of their aircraft being a pontoon, which had been converted into a makeshift life raft, discovered near Tromso in Norway. Nobile was found and rescued by a second rescue mission, but Amundsen, fifty-five at the time, was lost forever.

So ended the life of one of polar exploration's most single-minded men. A born explorer, Amundsen died in a part of the world he had done much to open up. His determination to explore the frozen wastes led to much new scientific knowledge of the polar regions. The first man to set foot at the South Pole, the first man to sail the North West Passage, the first man to fly over the North Pole by dirigible, Amundsen did more than any other man to further Polar exploration. This is his story.

Campbell McCutcheon

MY LIFE
AS AN
EXPLORER

CHAPTER I

Early Memories

How did I happen to become an explorer? It did not just happen, for my career has been a steady progress toward a definite goal since I was fifteen years of age. Whatever I have accomplished in exploration has been the result of lifelong planning, painstaking preparation, and the hardest kind of conscientious work.

I was born a few miles south of Oslo in Norway, and when I was three months of age my parents removed to the capital, where I was reared and educated.

I passed without incident through the usual educational routine of Norway, which is divided into a primary school for the ages of six to nine, a "gymnasium" for the ages of nine to fifteen, and college from the age of fifteen to eighteen. My father died when I was fourteen, and my older brothers went out into the world to care for themselves. I was thus left at home alone with my mother, by whom I was directed toward a course to prepare me to practise medicine. This ambition, however – which originated with her and for which I never shared her enthusiasm – was never to be realized. When I was fifteen years old, the works of Sir John Franklin, the great British explorer, fell into my hands. I read them with a fervid fascination which has shaped the whole course of my life. Of all the brave Britishers who for 400 years had given freely of their treasure, courage, and enterprise to dauntless but unsuccessful attempts to negotiate the Northwest Passage, none was braver than Sir John Franklin. His description of the return from one of his expeditions thrilled me as nothing I had ever read before. He told how for three weeks he and his little band had battled with the ice and storms, with no food to eat except a few bones found at a deserted Indian camp, and how before they finally returned to the outpost of civilization they were reduced to eating their own boot leather to keep themselves alive.

Strangely enough the thing in Sir John's narrative that appealed to me most strongly was the sufferings he and his men endured. A strange ambition burned within me to endure those same sufferings. Perhaps the idealism of youth, which often takes a turn toward martyrdom, found its crusade in me in the form of Arctic exploration. I, too, would suffer in a cause-not in the blazing desert on the way to Jerusalem, but in the frozen North on the way to new knowledge in the unpierced unknown.

In any event, Sir John's descriptions decided me upon my career. Secretly – because I would never have dared to mention the idea to my mother, who I knew would be unsympathetic – I irretrievably decided to be an Arctic explorer.

More than that, I began at once to fit myself for this career. In Norway, in those days, there were no organized athletic sports as there are now everywhere. The only sports at all were football and skiing. Although I did not like football, I went in for it as part of the task of training my body to endure hardship. But to skiing I took with perfect naturalness and intense enthusiasm. At every opportunity of freedom from school, from November to April, I went out in the open, exploring the hills and mountains which rise in every direction around Oslo, increasing my skill in traversing ice and snow and hardening my muscles for the coming great adventure.

In those days, houses were kept tightly closed in winter, so I was regarded as an innovator and something of a freak because I insisted on sleeping with my bedroom windows wide open, even in the bitterest weather. My mother anxiously expostulated with me about this practice. To her I explained that I liked fresh air, but of course it was really a part of my conscientious hardening process.

At eighteen I graduated from the college, and, in pursuance of my mother's ambition for me, entered the university, taking up the medical course. Like all fond mothers, mine believed that I was a paragon of industry, but the truth is that I was a worse than indifferent student. Her death two years later, in my twenty-first year, saved her from the sad discovery which she otherwise would have made, that my own ambitions lay in another direction and that I had made but poor progress in realizing hers. With enormous relief, I soon left the university, to throw myself whole-heartedly into the dream of my life.

Before I could realize it, however, I had to discharge the duty of all young men in Norway, of performing my tour of military service. This I was eager to do, both because I wanted to be a good citizen and because I felt that military training would be of great benefit to me as further preparation for life. I had, however, one serious disqualification for a military career, which was unsuspected by most of my companions. My eyesight was especially powerful, but I was troubled by near-sightedness, which, to this day, though gradually improved, is not wholly corrected. If this defect were discovered by the medical examiner, I would not be admitted to military training. Fortunately, I had refused to wear the glasses that had been prescribed for me.

When the day came for me to take my physical examination for the army, I was ushered into an office where the chief examiner sat behind a desk with two assistants. He was an elderly physician, and, as I quickly discovered, to my extreme embarrassment, an enthusiastic student of the human body. I was, of course, stripped to the skin for the examination. The old doctor looked me over and at once burst into loud exclamations over my physical development. Evidently my eight years of conscientious exercise had not been without their effect. He said to me: "Young man, how in the world did you ever develop such a splendid set of muscles?" I explained that I had always been fond of exercise and had taken a great deal of it. So delighted was the old gentleman at his discovery, which he appeared to regard as extraordinary, that he called to a group of officers in the adjoining room to come in and view the novelty. Needless to say, I was embarrassed almost to extinction by this exhibition of my person in the altogether.

The incident, however, had its fortunate side. In his enthusiasm over the rest of my physical equipment, the good old doctor entirely forgot to examine my eyes. Consequently, I was passed with flying colours and got my training in the army.

Military service in Norway occupies only a few weeks of the year, so I had plenty of time to carry on my own course of special training for my future career of explorer. One incident of this training very nearly wrote "finis" to my life, and involved dangers and hardships fully as severe as any I was destined ever to encounter in the polar regions.

This adventure happened in my twenty-second year. It was in an effort to achieve a sort of Arctic passage not many miles from Oslo itself. To the west of the capital there rises a line of steep mountain sides surmounted by a plateau of about six thousand feet elevation. This plateau extends westward nearly to the coast of Norway, in the neighbourhood of Bergen, and is marked on that side by an even more abrupt descent – so difficult, in fact, that only two safe trails down its side exist. In summer the plateau was frequented only by Lapp herdsmen pasturing their nomadic herds of reindeer. No farmers lived there, so the only building of any sort in many miles was a hut erected by these herdsmen for shelter from cold rainstorms in the fall of the year. In the winter, the Lapps descended to the valleys, and the plateau was deserted. There was no record of any person having ever crossed the plateau in winter, from the mountain farm called Mogen on the east to the farm called Garen on the west coast. I determined to make this crossing.

Choosing a single companion, I proposed that we make the venture together. He agreed, and we left Oslo during the Christmas holidays. We made our way rapidly over the snow on our skis to the little farm called Mogen. Here we stopped at the last farmhouse that we expected to see on the whole trip. It was a tiny affair of only one room in which were crowded an old man and his wife and their two married sons-six people in all. They were, of course, of the simplest peasant type. There were no tourists in those days in any season of the year, so that our descent upon them would have been a surprise at any time. Coming as we did in the dead of winter, they were doubly astonished. We had no difficulty in persuading them to allow us to stay overnight with them. They were hospitable folk and made room for us on the floor near the fireplace, where we rolled ourselves up in our reindeer sleeping bags and slept very comfortably.

On the morrow, however, it was snowing, and this storm turned out to be a regular blizzard. It lasted for eight days, and we spent the whole of this time in the farmhouse.

Of course, our hosts were curious to know what errand could have brought us to their remote home. When we told them our plan to ascend to the plateau and cross it to the coast, they were first incredulous and then greatly alarmed for our safety. All three of the men were familiar with the plateau and joined in earnestly warning us not to attempt to cross it in winter. It had never been done, and they were sure it could not be done. Nevertheless, we were determined to push on and attempt it, so on the ninth day they accompanied us to the foot of the plateau at the head of their valley and showed us the best way to ascend. They bade us good-bye sadly, and we understood that they feared they would never see us again. Of course, we were light-hearted about the enterprise. To us it seemed simple enough. The plateau was only about seventy-two English miles wide, and with our skill on skis and any decent luck with the weather, we counted at most on two days to make the crossing. Our equipment for the venture was based upon this theory, and accordingly was of the sketchiest character. Besides our skis and ski sticks, we each had a reindeer sleeping bag that we carried on our backs. We took no tent. Each of us had a small bag containing our provisions and a small alcohol lamp. This bag was rolled inside the sleeping bag. Our provisions consisted of a few crackers, some bars of chocolate, and a little butter – at the best scant rations for perhaps eight days. We had a pocket compass and a map of the region printed on paper.

We had no difficulty in ascending to the plateau. It was not a perfectly level plain that we found, but, for the practical purpose of travel, it might as well have been, for it offered no distinguishing landmarks to guide our course. There was nothing to be seen but an endless succession of small and indistinct hills.

We set our course by the compass. Our destination for our first day's travel was the herder's hut which was about in the middle of the plateau. At that time of the year in Norway, the daylight is little better than twilight, but with our compass we had no difficulty in getting along, and early in the evening we found the hut.

Our elation at this discovery was rather short-lived, for we found that the door and window of the hut had been nailed up and the top of the chimney covered over with

18

heavy boards. We were pretty well tired with our day's exertions, the wind had started to blow again, and the thermometer was about ten degrees Fahrenheit below zero. With these handicaps, it was the hardest kind of work to get into the hut and later to clamber on to the roof and clear the top of the chimney so that we could start a fire. Both of us got our fingers badly frostbitten, and my companion, for some weeks after, was in grave danger of losing one of his.

We had the good fortune to find firewood stacked up in the hut. It took us some time, however, to make it of any use to us-if you have ever tried to build an open fire under a cold chimney with the thermometer below zero, you will understand the difficulty we had in getting a draught going. The cold air settles down on your fire like a blanket, and you have to get a pretty brisk blaze going before the heat displaces the column of cold air in the flue. Meanwhile, of course, in our efforts to do this, we had filled the little hut with smoke that got into our eyes and throats and caused us much discomfort.

We felt pretty good after we had the fire blazing and had eaten a supper. At length, we rolled up in our sleeping bags in the bunks on the opposite wall and slept very comfortably.

In the morning, we found that our troubles had only begun. The wind of the night before was still blowing, and it was now snowing heavily. The storm was so severe that it would obviously be folly to venture out in it. We therefore settled down to sit the storm out before the fireplace. Further exploration of the hut revealed another bit of good luck – it disclosed a small sack of rye flour that had been left behind by some herdsman. As we now realized that our own provisions must be husbanded, we made a thin porridge of this flour, which we cooked in an iron kettle over the open fire. We spent two days in the hut, and the only food we took in that time was this weak porridge. At best, it was not very nourishing, and neither was it palatable.

On the third day, the storm had somewhat abated, and we decided to resume our march westward toward Garen. We now had to set our course very carefully, as there were only two places on the west coast at which a descent from the plateau was at all possible, and as these places were several miles apart, we had now definitely to choose one of them and reject the other. Having made this choice we set forward.

We had not gone far before it started snowing again and the weather grew milder. We had frequently to consult the map to take our bearings, and the wet snow falling on the flimsy paper soon reduced it to pulp. After that, we had to proceed as best we could by the compass alone.

Night overtook us before we reached the edge of the plateau and, of course, there was nothing to do but to camp where it found us, out in the open. That night nearly finished us. When we had unrolled our sleeping bags, we took out our provision bags and laid them at our feet. Alongside them we set up our ski sticks as markers to indicate in the morning where the bags were if the overnight snow should cover them. We spent the night in extreme discomfort. The soft snow had melted on our clothing and had saturated it with moisture. When we got into our sleeping bags, the heat of our bodies turned enough of this moisture into steam so that it permeated the inside of the sleeping bags as well. It was a wretched experience. Worse yet, it turned cold again in the night. I woke up in the darkness feeling half frozen, and was so uncomfortable that I could not go back to sleep. It finally occurred to me that, if I got up and drank some of the alcohol out of the lamp in my provision bag, it would restore my circulation. I climbed out of the sleeping bag and felt around in the dark until I got hold of my ski stick, and then I clawed about for my provision bag. To my astonishment and chagrin, it was not to be found. When morning broke, we both resumed the search and could find neither of the bags. To this day I have not been able to make a reasonable conjecture that would explain what became of them. There was, however, no doubt of the fact – they were gone.

Our plight now was worse than uncomfortable, it was extremely dangerous. Unless we could speedily reach shelter and food, we should certainly freeze to death. With this alarming situation confronting us, we headed west again in hopes of reaching the edge of the plateau before night fell.

Luck was still against us. It soon began to snow so heavily that we could not see our way more than a few feet ahead. We decided now that the only thing to do was to turn around and try to make our way east across the plateau to our starting point. We made a few miles on this new course when night again over took us.

Again the night was wet. We were drenched, and our bags were still heavy with moisture. Snow was still falling. When night came on, we had reached a small peak that thrust up out of the plateau. We sought out its lee side, figuring that we might be reasonably comfortable if we could keep out of the wind. We found that it did make a good deal of difference. I decided to improve even on that. I dug into the snow and made myself a small cave not much larger than my body, and into the cave I climbed head first and pulled my bag in after me. I soon conratulated myself on this idea, for I escaped altogether the gusts of wind outside.

In the night, the weather turned cold suddenly. The wet snow had settled down on me in my cave and over its entrance at my feet. When the temperature dropped, it froze. In the middle of the night I woke up. I was lying on my back with my right wrist across , my eyes and the palm of my hand up – as one often sleeps to keep the morning light out of his eyes. My muscles felt cramped and I made the instinctive move to change my position. I could not move an inch. I was practically frozen inside a solid block of ice! I struggled desperately to free myself, but without the slightest effect. I shouted to my companion. Of course he could not hear.

I was now stricken with horror. In my panic, I naturally thought he likewise had been frozen in the wet snow that had fallen in the night and that he was in a like predicament with me. Unless a thaw immediately set in, we should both soon freeze to death in our ghastly coffins of ice.

My shouts quickly died away, as I found it impossible to breathe deeply. I realized that I must keep quiet or I would suffocate. I do not know whether it was the heaviness of the little air I had to breathe, or what was the reason, but I soon dropped off into either sleep or unconsciousness. When I came to I could hear faint sounds. My companion, after all, had not been imprisoned. Probably the only reason he had not emulated my example and built himself a cave the night before was that he was too tired, and from exhaustion too indifferent, to go to the trouble. In any event, his failure to do so saved both our lives. When he awakened and looked about, he found himself alone in an ocean of snow. He called to me, and I did not answer. Then he began a frantic search for some trace that would show him where I had gone. There was only one, and providentially his eye fell upon it – a few hairs of the reindeer skin of my sleeping bag were visible in the snow. At once he began digging with his hands and ski stick to extricate me from my prison. It took him three hours to dig me out.

Both of us were now getting pretty weak. It was still night when he got me out, but we were too much upset to think of trying to rest further. Though it was still dark, the sky was clear and we were able to set a course and travel by the stars. We had been going two hours, with my companion in the lead, when suddenly he disappeared as if the earth had swallowed him up. Instinctively, I realized that he had gone over a precipice, and, instinctively, I acted instantly to save myself. I threw myself flat on the ground. A moment later, I heard his voice calling up, "Don't move. I have dropped over a precipice." He had indeed fallen about thirty feet. Fortunately, he had landed on his back, so that the sleeping bag which he carried as a pack on his shoulders had broken the force of the fall and he did not suffer more than a severe shaking up. Naturally, we did not attempt to go farther until daylight. Then we ploughed ahead on our seemingly hopeless travels.

We had now been four days without food of any sort, and the two days before that our diet of weak rye porridge had not been much better, so far as sustenance was concerned. We were getting nearly exhausted. The only thing that had saved us from collapse was our ability to get drinking water. On the plateau were numerous little lakes connected by small streams, and at these streams we had been able to keep our stomachs filled with water, and this saved us from the extreme effects of starvation.

At nightfall we came upon a little shanty filled with hay. There were ski tracks around the shanty. This discovery renewed our courage and proved that we were certainly back near civilization. It gave us hope, that, if we could keep ourselves going, on the morrow we might find food and shelter. The hay offered us a luxurious bed, and we spent the night burrowed into the heart of it.

The next morning I turned out to explore our surroundings. My companion was now so exhausted and dispirited that he seemed unequal to the effort and I left him in the haymow while I followed the ski tracks. After an hour's trudging, I saw a man in the distance. I surmised correctly that he was a peasant farmer making the morning rounds of the snares he had set for ptarmigan. I called loudly to him. He gave a startled look and, to my dismay, proceeded to run as fast as he could away from me. These lonely peasants are a superstitious folk. While they are courageous enough in the presence of real danger, they suffer many terrors of their own creation. Doubtless his first impression of me was of a ghostly apparition haunting the uninhabited plateau.

I called again and threw my whole soul into the cry. My tone must have conveyed my desperation, for the man stopped running and, after some hesitation, came back to meet me. I explained our plight and asked him where we were. I had a little difficulty in understanding his explanation, and even when I did, could hardly believe my senses, for it showed that we were now not more than an hour's travel from the farmhouse above Mogen from which, eight days before, we had started on our misadventure.

Heartened by this information, I hurried back for my companion. The news put fresh vigour in him, too, and soon, with no great trouble, we made our way down the little valley to the familiar farmhouse. We knocked at the door, were invited to enter, and went in. I was puzzled at our reception—until later I saw myself in the mirror. In the single room of the farmhouse the women were busy at their spinning and the men at wood-carving. They looked up hospitably, but merely greeted us with a brief "How do you do," in an entirely impersonal and inquiring manner. It was soon apparent that they did not recognize us. Little wonder, as I later realized, for our scraggly beards had grown, our eyes were gaunt and hollow, our cheeks were sunken, and the ruddy glow of colour had changed to a ghastly greenish yellow. We were a truly awful spectacle. Our hosts at first would not believe us when we explained that we were the two young fellows who had left them eight days earlier. They could see no resemblance to their former guests in the gaunt spectres before them. At length we convinced them, and they showed us every kindness. We spent a couple of days with them, eating and sleeping until our strength returned, and then, with many expressions of gratitude, we took our leave of them and made our way safe into Oslo.

The sequel of the story I did not myself learn until a year later, when I discovered it was known that the farmer who owned Garen, on the westerly edge of the plateau at the head of the trail we had intended to descend, had come out of his house one morning and found ski tracks within a few yards of his doorway coming from the east and not from the west. He could not credit his eyes, because he knew no one had ever come that way in the winter, nor did he believe it was possible. Those tracks could have been none other than ours, for the date also matched.

Think of it! We had been unknowingly within a hundred yards of our destination and had turned back to recross the plateau after being within ten minutes' walk of a safe haven on its western edge!

As I said when I started to describe this adventure, it involved as many hardships and dangers as anything I later encountered in my polar expeditions. It was a part of my preliminary training for my polar career. The training proved severer than the experience for which it was a preparation, and it well-nigh ended the career before it began.

CHAPTER II

Ice-bound In The Antarctic

As Soon as my army training was over, I undertook the next step in my preparation for Arctic exploration. By this time I had read all the books on the subject I could lay my hands on, and I had been struck by one fatal weakness common to many of the preceding Arctic expeditions. This was that the commanders of these expeditions had not always been ships' captains. They had almost invariably relied for the navigation of their vessels upon the services of experienced skippers. The fatal defect of this practice had been in every case that, once embarked at sea, the expedition had not one leader but two. Invariably this resulted in a division of responsibility between the commander and the skipper, incessant friction, divided counsels, and a lowered morale for the subordinate members of the expedition. Always two factions developed – one comprising the commander and the scientific staff, the other comprising the captain and the crew. I was resolved, therefore, that I should never lead an expedition until I was prepared to remedy this defect. The only way to remedy it was to equip myself with experience as a skipper and actually to qualify as a ship's captain. I could then lead my expeditions both as explorer and navigator and avoid this division into two factions.

To gain a skipper's license, however, I must get several years of actual experience as a member of the crew under a qualified captain. For this reason, during the summers of 1894-96, I signed as a sailor aboard a sailing ship. This not only gave me the opportunity to work up to the position of mate and prepare for an examination for a skipper's license, but also took me into my beloved Arctic, where my experiences were also a preparation for the future I had in mind.

In 1897, I had the good fortune to be accepted for membership in the ship's company of the Belgian Antarctic Expedition to study the South Magnetic Pole. Though I was only twenty-five years old, I was chosen first mate before the *Belgica* left Europe. The expedition was decidedly an international affair. The commander was a Belgian sailor. The captain was a Belgian artillery officer who had served in the French navy and who had become a first-rate skipper. The first mate was myself. Dr Cook, of later polar fame, was the ship's physician. The chief scientist was a Rumanian. The second scientist was a Pole. Five members of the crew were Norwegians. The rest were Belgians.

The South Magnetic Pole is on the Antarctic continent, far south of Australia in the South Pacific Ocean. However, the plan of our commander was to proceed, not by way of Australia, but by way of Cape Horn. We reached the Strait of Magellan in the winter of 1897, which, of course, in that latitude, was the summer of the year. We proceeded south to Tierra del Fuego. In those days, little was known of this region scientifically, and our commander was so taken with the possibilities of discovery there that we lingered for several weeks, gathering specimens of its natural history, mapping its shores, and taking meteorological observations. This delay had serious consequences which will appear shortly.

Proceeding farther south, we passed the South Shetland Islands and came in view of the Antarctic continent, which in this region is known as Graham's Land. This region, too,

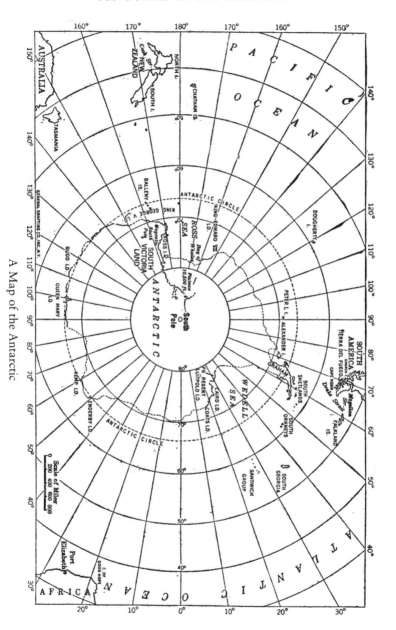

A Map of the Antarctic

was partly unmapped, and we spent some time here tracing the outlines of the coast, and emerged at the south end of a passage through it into the Pacific Ocean.

By this time, winter was drawing near, and we had still a considerable distance to go to reach our destination south of Australia. We therefore headed west, and soon had an adventure that came near ending the career of all of us. One day, when I came to the bridge to relieve the captain for the afternoon watch, I found we were battling with a terrific gale, accompanied by sleet and snow. Icebergs were visible in all directions. The captain pointed to one not far distant to the north and explained that he had been manoeuvring all through the watch to keep the ship in the lee of this berg, which, by sheltering us from the heaviest of the wind and the swells, saved us from being driven off our course. His instructions to me were to continue these manoeuvres until I should be relieved for the night watch, and to pass them on to my successor. This I did, transmitting the instructions to the young Belgian who took the watch. When I turned into my bunk, I could feel the ship rolling in response to the swell, which, however, was not the tremendous heave of the main Pacific, but was a modified rolling of the current which came around the iceberg to us. I was rocked to sleep by this rolling motion. Imagine my astonishment when I awoke in the morning and found the ship dead becalmed! Certain that something extraordinary had happened, I hastened into my clothes and hurried to the bridge. There I found that we were in a small basin, icelocked on every side by a complete circle of towering icebergs. I asked the young Belgian how in the world we ever got into this place. His response was that he had no more idea of how it happened than I myself. In the darkness of the night and the driving snowstorm, he had been unable to keep the iceberg in view, and the ship had been driven aimlessly by the wind, with the result that it had been lifted on one of the mighty Pacific swells through an opening between two icebergs and had landed us in the becalmed basin where we now lay. Nothing short of a miracle of coincidence had saved us from being dashed to pieces by the bergs that formed the shallow entrance we had hurdled on the back of that swelling wave.

At the best, though we had enjoyed this much good fortune, we were in perhaps an even greater danger than before. It was all very well to escape death by breaking up on the berg, but now we were confronted with the possibility of death by being caught irrevocably within a ring of bergs. Fortunately for us, by very careful manoeuvring, we succeeded in extricating ourselves.

We had not gone far, however, when the danger we had just escaped threatened us in a yet more serious form, not by blind accident as before, but by reason of a lack of experience in Polar navigation. Skirting the Antarctic ice field on our westward way, we encountered another terrific gale blowing from the north. We were in imminent danger of being blown against the wall of ice that lay to the south of us. The instinct of any navigator accustomed to the Polar seas would have been to use every effort to get away to the north and into the open sea. This we could have done. But at this juncture my two superior officers saw an opening in the ice field to the south of us and decided to ride before the storm into this opening.

They could not have made a greater mistake. I saw and understood fully the great danger they exposed the whole expedition to, but I was not asked for my opinion, and discipline required me to keep silent. The thing I most feared happened. By the time we had ridden out of the storm, we were probably more than a hundred miles within the ice field. We awoke one morning to find the ice lane we had travelled had closed behind us. Here we were, fast in the Antarctic ice drifting round in the uncharted southern seas at the beginning of the long Polar winter.

Our position was even more perilous than this sounds, because we were not equipped for a winter's stay in Antarctic regions. The original plan of our expedition had been to proceed during the summer to the region of the South Magnetic Pole on South Victoria Land and there to establish a winter camp where four men would be left with adequate supplies while the ship and the rest of the men returned to civilization for the winter. They were to come back for their four comrades the following spring. The men who were to be left on the Antarctic continent were the Rumanian scientist, the Polish assistant, Dr Cook, and myself.

Now, however, the entire ship's company faced the prospect of a winter in the Antarctic with no winter clothing for the crew, without adequate provisions for so many men, and even without lamps enough to light the quarters of all. It was a truly dreadful prospect.

For thirteen months, we lay caught in the vise of this ice field. Two of the sailors went insane. Every member of the ship's company was afflicted with scurvy, and all but three of us were prostrated by it. This wholesale attack of scurvy was a sad experience. Both Dr Cook and I knew from our reading of Arctic travels that it could be avoided by the use of fresh meat. We had, therefore, spent many weary hours, after the day's hard work was done, travelling for miles over the ice in search of seals and penguins, and with great labour had killed and brought to the ship a great number of each. The commander, however, developed an aversion to the flesh of both that amounted almost to a mania. He was not content only to refuse to eat it himself, but he forbade any of the ship's company to indulge in it. Consequently, all of us soon got the scurvy. The commander and the captain were both so prostrated that they took to their beds and made their wills.

The command of the expedition now devolved upon me as ranking officer. About the first thing I did was to get out the few men that were able to work, and dig through the snow alongside the ship to the carcasses of the seals. Steaks were speedily cut from them, and the cook was ordered to thaw them out and prepare them. Everybody aboard eagerly ate his share, even the commander.

It was marvellous to see the change wrought by this simple change in diet. Within a week, all the men plainly showed an improvement in their condition.

It was in this fearful emergency, during these thirteen long months in which almost the certainty of death stared us steadily in the face, that I came to know Dr Cook intimately and to form the affection for him and the gratitude to him which nothing in his later career could ever cause me to alter. He, of all the ship's company, was the one man of unfaltering courage, unfailing hope, endless cheerfulness, and unwearied kindness. When anyone was sick, he was at his bedside to comfort him; when any was disheartened, he was there to encourage and inspire. And not only was his faith undaunted, but his ingenuity and enterprise were boundless. With the return of the sun after the long Antarctic night, he led small parties on scouting expeditions in all directions looking for evidences that the ice might providentially open and leave a channel for us back to the open sea.

One day, somebody in the party noticed that the melting ice had formed a small basin of water about a thousand yards from the ship. The rest of us thought nothing of it, as naturally water would form here and there. Somehow, though, to Dr Cook's restless mind this basin seemed an omen of hope. He declared his firm conviction that the ice would break, and that, when the opening came, it would lead to this basin. Therefore, he proposed what sounded at first like a mad enterprise: that we should cut a channel through the thousand yards of rough ice to this basin and float the *Belgica* through it, so that, if the crack came, the ship could take immediate advantage of it.

I say it seemed a mad undertaking for two reasons: first, the only things we had on board to cut ice with were a few four-foot saws and some explosives; secondly, most of the men were wholly unused to this kind of work and were weak and emaciated. Nevertheless, Dr Cook's confidence prevailed – at least it would give us something to do besides sitting and contemplating our probable fate. All hands, therefore, turned out, and the enterprise began.

A motley-looking crew they were. When the commander had taken to his bed with the scurvy, I had sized up the equipment of the men and realized that, except for four of us, they were most inadequately clad to stand a winter in the Antarctic. I had, therefore, rifled a carefully hoarded store of bright red blankets, had caused them to be cut up after a pattern, and sewed into loose suits for the men. These suits provided sufficient warmth, but when the men appeared on deck with them they certainly produced a bizarre and theatrical effect.

We marked our proposed channel through the ice and fell to work. With the saws, we cut triangular lines in the ice and then applied a stick of dynamite to blow the cakes loose. We found that the cakes had a tendency to cling to the edges in spite of the explosive. Dr Cook then invented an ingenious scheme of cutting off one point of the triangle, which had the effect of freeing the cake at the time of explosion.

Weary weeks we spent at this labour, but finally the job was done, and we went to bed one night planning to tow the ship to the basin the following morning. Imagine our horror on awakening . to discover that the pressure from the surrounding ice pack had driven the banks of our channel together, and we were locked in as fast as ever.

Our dejection was turned to joy shortly after, however, when a shift of wind opened the channel again. We now lost no time in towing the ship into the basin.

Now that we were here, we seemed no nearer escape than before. Other weary weeks passed us by. Then the miracle happened – exactly what Cook had predicted. The ice opened and the lane to the sea ran directly through our basin! Joy restored our energy, and with all speed we made our way to the open sea and safety.

Our perils, however, were not yet past. Before we could emerge into open water, we were compelled to pass between two giant icebergs, and for several days we were again held as in a vise between them. All day and all night we were subjected to a terrific grinding pressure, and the noise of ice cakes battering against our sides and splintering off incessantly was at times so loud as to make conversation trying. Here again Dr Cook's ingenuity saved the day. He had carefully preserved the skins of the penguins we had killed, and we now made them into mats and lowered them over the sides of the vessel, where they took up and largely mitigated the impact of the ice.

Even after we had made the open sea, some danger beset us. Our chronometer had shared the shocks of many a blow from the ice which had shaken the ship as though it were an earthquake. For this reason, we could not be sure of the accuracy of the observations we took to determine our exact latitude and longitude. Navigation back to civilization, therefore, was a little bit uncertain. Fortunately, at length, the welcome cry of "Land!" was heard from the crow's nest. Certainly we were approaching the Strait of Magellan.

But here a new perplexity arose. Where was the channel? In those days, the numerous islands and bays in this region were not so well mapped as they now are, and, with the uncertainty as to our exact position, we were not at first sure what part of the region we were in. Soon, however, we clearly identified Church Island by its striking likeness in appearance to a church, from which its name was derived. I will not detail the perils that beset us in working our way through the Strait. We took refuge in the lee of Church Island, dragged our anchors, and nearly went on the rocks of a neighbouring island. Starting round the coast, we steered into what later turned out to be a blind alley, where we certainly should have been driven on the rocks by a westerly gale; but we discovered our mistake with only about a minute to spare, and tacked around a foaming reef, which we escaped by inches, into the true channel. At length, after a weary voyage, we returned to Europe, arriving in 1899, two years after our departure.

The following year I got my skipper's license and then began making definite plans for my first expedition. Dr Fridtjof Nansen, whose daring exploits in the *Fram* had made him the idol of my boyhood, was the Grand Old Man of Arctic exploration in Norway. I knew that a word of encouragement from him would be priceless to me in enlisting aid in my enterprise; on the other hand, a word of disparagement from him would be fatal. I went, therefore, to see him and laid before him my plans and hopes and asked his benediction. This he graciously gave; and he even went further-he offered to commend me to the good offices of people who might help me.

Immensely encouraged by this interview, I next determined to pursue studies in magnetic science and in the methods of taking magnetic observations. My expedition must have a scientific purpose as well as the purpose of exploration. Otherwise I should not be taken seriously and would not get backing.

I wrote, therefore, to the Director of the British Observatory at Kew, asking permission to go there and pursue these studies. The Director of the Observatory refused my request.

I now turned to the Director of the Meteorological Observatory at Oslo. From him I got a card of introduction to the Director of Deutsche Seewarte at Hamburg. Armed with this, I went to the great German seaport and hired a cheap room in a poor quarter of the city. My funds were low and I had to conserve them.

My prospects of getting an interview with the distinguished Geheimrath George von Neumayer were, to say the least, not very bright. I was unknown to him and was an utterly undistinguished stranger. However, I was desperate and had to take desperate measures. With beating heart, I presented myself at his outer office and handed in my card of introduction.

In a short time, to my great gratification, I was ushered into his presence. I beheld a man of probably seventy years, whose white hair, benign, clean-shaven face, and gentle eyes presented a most striking resemblance to the famous musician, Franz Liszt. He greeted me cordially and asked me my business. I eagerly explained that I intended to be an explorer on my own account, that I had had two years' experience with an Antarctic expedition, and that I must learn how to take magnetic observations so that I might acquire scientific data to justify my adventure. The old gentleman listened kindly but finally exclaimed: "Young man, you have something more on your mind than this! Tell me what it is."

I told him of my ambition to be the first to conquer the Northwest Passage. Still he was not satisfied. "Ah," he exclaimed, " there is still more." Then I told him I wanted to make the conclusive observations of the true location of the North Magnetic Pole. When I said this, he rose eagerly, came over to me, and threw his arms around me in a warm embrace. "Young man," he said, "if you do that, you will be the benefactor of mankind for ages to come. That is the great adventure."

His kindness for the next three months well-nigh overwhelmed me. A bachelor and a man of comfortable means, he lived in a good hotel down town, and frequently he insisted upon my dining with him there. To me this hotel seemed like a palace. Its dining room was a fairyland of savoury delights, and its menu a Lucullian feast. More than this, the good old Geheimrath would include me in dinners that he gave to visiting scientists, and thereby provided me, not only with a much-appreciated meal, but with the stimulation of contact with active minds and intellects of achievement. Never shall I cease to be grateful to this kindly old soul who so greatly encouraged and helped me. I tried to repay his interest by being every day the first to arrive at the observatory in the morning and the last to leave at night. I proceeded in my study with indefatigable zeal, and in a few months had gained a working knowledge of the theory and practice of magnetic observations.

When I had finished at Hamburg, his good offices procured me access to the observatory at Wilhelmshaven and also at Potsdam.

In 1900, I bought the ship for this my first expedition. She was a small fishing smack from the northern part of Norway. She was forty-seven tons and of the same age as myself. The following summer I spent with my precious fishing smack in the North Atlantic between Norway and Greenland, taking oceanographic observations in that region. I knew that Dr Nansen wanted this data for his own use, and I was determined to get it for him as a mark of my gratitude to him. He was delighted when I returned in the fall and presented the data to him.

The winter and spring of 1902-1903 I spent in feverish preparation for my great adventure of the Northwest Passage. I besieged every possible source of funds – the learned societies and the private patrons of science. The rest of my time was spent in selecting and ordering supplies.

Despair almost overcame me at times, because, in spite of everything, sufficient funds were not forthcoming. Some of the more impatient men from whom I had got supplies began pressing me for payment. Finally, on the morning of June 16, 1903, I was confronted with a supreme crisis. The most important of my creditors angrily demanded payment within twenty-four hours, with the threat that he would libel my vessel and cause my arrest for fraud. The ruin of my years of work seemed imminent. I grew desperate and I resolved upon a desperate expedient. I summoned my six carefully chosen companions, explained my predicament, and asked if they would cooperate with me in my strategy. They enthusiastically agreed. Therefore, at midnight on June 16th, in the midst of a perfect deluge of rain, we seven conspirators made our way to the wharf where the *Gjoa* was tied, went aboard, cast off the hawsers, and turned southward toward the Skagger Rack and the North Sea. When dawn arose on our truculent creditor, we were safely out on the open main, seven as light-hearted pirates as ever flew the black flag, disappearing upon a quest that should take us three years and on which we were destined to succeed in an enterprise that had baffled our predecessors for four centuries. That, however, is another story for another chapter.

CHAPTER III

The Conquest Of
The Northwest Passage

At Last! The great adventure for which my whole life had been a preparation was under way! The Northwest Passage – that baffling mystery to all the navigators of the past – was at last to be ours!

Our first stop was at Godhavn on Disco Island, on the west coast of Greenland. Here we took on twenty dogs that were supplied to us by the Royal Danish Greenland Trading Company. Pressing on to the north, we made Dalrymple Rock, an ancient rendezvous of the Scottish whaling fleet. We had arranged with the Scottish Whaling Company for a supply of gasoline to be taken on at this point, besides provisions to replenish the stores we had used up crossing the Atlantic.

Now, a passage from Godhavn to Dalrymple Rock sounds simple enough to say, but between these two points lies Melville Bay, which is a most difficult stretch of water to navigate. Drifting ice and heavy winds complicate the job. However, with great difficulty, we finally rounded Cape York, made Dalrymple Rock, took on our supplies, and headed westward.

Surely the Arctic Seas have seldom seen such a spectacle as we presented. The *Gjoa* was 72 feet long, 11 feet wide, and of shallow draught. Naturally, we had only one mast, which gave us one mainsail and a couple of jibs. We had a

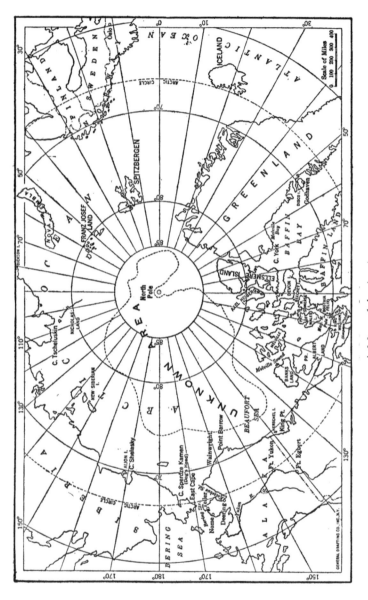

A Map of the Arctic

good auxiliary motor, though in those days gasoline engines were still so uncertain that we had been gravely criticized for risking the dangers of explosion and fire when I had the motor installed.

So far there was no great novelty in our appearance. But such a cargo! First of all, every square inch of space in the hold had been carefully calculated and our packing cases made to fit so that when we got them all stowed there was not a wasted square foot of space left. This cargo weighed the *Gjoa* nearly to the water's edge. But the hold would not contain all the supplies we must carry. Consequently, almost the entire deck was likewise piled high with boxes, so that when we steamed into the Arctic Ocean we looked like a moving-van afloat!

Our appearance, however, gave us no concern. We were too delighted at being safely on our way, with everything we needed for several years' absence. Our first station was made at Beechy Island which lies north of North Somerset Island. Here we took a series of careful magnetic observations to find out in which direction the Magnetic Pole really was. The observations indicated the west coast of Boothia Felix. This confirmed, we entered Peel Strait. We had now arrived at the southernmost point reached by earlier navigators in this region, our predecessor having been Sir Alan Young, who attained this latitude in the ship *Pandora* in the year 1875.

Here, we had three adventures, each one of which threatened to end our careers forever. The first was caused by the extraordinary formation of the ocean bed in this region. We had no charts to go by, so had constantly to resort to soundings. On one side of our narrow craft the lead would show an astonishing depth, while on the other the jagged rocks could be seen near the surface. Feeling our way through the treacherous channel (of course, none of these waters was then charted), we had the bad luck to run suddenly on a hidden rock. It seemed for a time as if we had certainly met our finish, but a little later a heavy swell carried us off. Our joy on discovering we had not sprung a leak was short-lived, for the helmsman suddenly called to me at my station in the crow's nest that the rudder would not answer to the spin of the wheel. A quick investigation showed that, in sliding off the rock, the rudder had been struck squarely on the bottom with such force as to drive it upward and disengage the metal pins at top and bottom from the horizontal rings in which they normally rest. The pins, instead of fitting into the rings, were now poised on the edge of them. If the rudder were now pushed backward or to the side, they would come clear off and we should be drifting rudderless in the Arctic! But, to our immense relief, in a few minutes the pins dropped back into the rings, the rudder again responded to the wheel, and we were safe – but it was a very close call indeed.

Our escape from our second adventure was the result of the merest accident of good fortune. The little engine room in which our little gasoline motor was installed had been tightly packed with tanks of gasoline, leaving barely room for the engineer to move about his motor. One morning the engineer came to me and said that one of the tanks was leaking slightly – nothing serious, but if the leak were not checked, the room would ultimately become saturated with gasoline and the fumes might be dangerous. I investigated and suggested that he pump the contents of the leaking tank into another tank. Fortunately, he followed this suggestion at once: In the evening, we anchored under a small island. When I was about to turn in, I heard a terrible shout: "Fire!" All of us rushed on deck. Big flames came up from the engine room, and when we looked down into the room it was a mass of flames. The only thing we could do was to throw down water on it and after a time subdued the fire. On investigation, we found that the metal pipe of the empty tank had been broken off during our battle with the fire. If the engineer had not obeyed my order as quickly as he did, the contents of the leaking tank would have been spouted out into the fire. The result would have been an explosion with the loss of all.

Our third adventure was with a terrific gale which blew with unabated violence for four days from the west. In spite of anchors and engine, it seemed inevitable that we should be driven ashore on Boothia. So certain did this appear that I manoeuvred the *Gjoa* into a position facing the most likely looking bit of beach we could see, intending, if everything failed us, to drive bow on at full speed up this beach so that we would possibly be saved from smashing up and would be in the most favourable position for later efforts to drag the vessel back into the water. Fortunately, however, when the storm abated on the fourth day we were still holding our own and escaped with our ship whole.

It was now the 9th of September, and the Arctic night was drawing on. I knew we must find winter quarters. Cruising about in Rae Strait, we came to the south coast of King William Island. Here we found the most beautiful little landlocked bay that the heart of a sailor could desire. High hills surrounding it on all sides would shelter us from the gales. Nothing could have been more ideal for our purpose, so the *Gjoa* was speedily brought inside, and we began our preparations for a permanent camp.

Soon our cases were all on shore and unpacked. These cases were an essential part of our equipment and were a result of careful planning. They were made of boards cut from the most carefully selected lumber, all of a size, and were held together by copper nails. In those days copper was not as expensive as it now is, but at best this was an expensive construction. The point was, however, our cases should be nonmagnetic so that we could use them in building our magnetic observatories. Iron nails would affect the magnetic needles.

I have forgotten to mention that we had bought from the Germans a complete set of the most modern and accurate instruments for making our observations. These instruments were operated by a clock mechanism and were self-registering. A tiny beam of light, transmitted synchronously by the slightest vibration of the instrument needles, traced a photographic record on a slowly moving film. It was, therefore, necessary that our observatories should be lightproof as well as non-magnetic. This called for some ingenuity in construction but we succeeded admirably.

We had even brought with us slabs of marble on which to mount the instruments with perfect precision. These were laid with great care on a firm rock foundation in the base of the observatories, and, trenches were dug around the outside to drain off quickly any water that might be near during the summer thaw, so that by no chance could the foundations be undermined and the position of the instruments changed.

After we got our observatories built and our instruments installed, we built kennels for our dogs. When all was done, we could not have been more snugly housed anywhere in civilization. Our house was warm and weatherproof and we had every convenience we needed.

Our next concern was to lay in a supply of fresh meat. We went out in parties of two, hunting caribou, and soon had piled up a hundred carcasses.

One day, two of the boys and I were standing on the deck when one of them exclaimed: "There is a caribou!" He pointed to a small black object just on the skyline of one of the encircling hills. The other man, who had the best vision of the three, looked steadfastly at the black object for a moment and then turned to his companion and said: "That caribou walks on two legs." Sure enough, close scrutiny confirmed his quick perception that this was not a caribou but an Eskimo. Some other "two-legged caribous" joined the first, until five figures were outlined against the sky. Then they advanced toward us in a body. I sent the two boys for their rifles, and then the three of us advanced to meet them. I was in the lead and behind me came my little army of two. As the Eskimos neared us, we could see they were all armed with bows and arrows.

This began to look like a ticklish situation. We had no way of knowing whether their intentions were friendly or hostile. Certainly, they were equipped for war. However, there was nothing to do but meet them face to face. The two parties proceeded to within about fifteen paces and then halted. I then turned to my "army" and instructed them ostentatiously to throw their rifles on the ground. I then turned to the Eskimos. Their leader, seeing this pacific move, imitated it by turning to his followers and uttering a command. They obeyed by throwing their bows and arrows on the ground. I was unarmed and advanced toward them. The Eskimo leader also came out alone.

It is remarkable how accurately two men can communicate who do not speak a word of a common language and whose whole experience of life seems utterly separated from each other's. Expressions of the face, nods and shakes of the head, gestures and tones of the voice, convey meaning with astonishing accuracy. By these means, I quickly convinced the Eskimo leader that I wished to be his friend, and he reciprocated my wish. Soon we were all friendly and I invited them down to our ship.

This was a truly thrilling moment in the lives of these poor savages. No one of them had ever seen a white man before, yet white men were a part of the legendary tradition of their tribe. Seventy-two years earlier, their grandfathers had met Sir James Clark Ross on almost this very ground. They had been amazed at the appearance of the English and hugely impressed with their marvellous equipment. To Eskimos, who had never before had in their possession a metal tool or weapon or a stick of wood the size of a man's hand (no driftwood floats in this region), the white man's knives, axes, guns, and sleds seemed miraculous. After a brief stay, Sir James and his men had gone, and never again did those Eskimos see a white man; but, naturally, to their children and their children's children the theme of many an evening tale was the marvel of the visit of these godlike white men. Therefore, to our present visitors our appearance was perhaps even more impressive, because to them it must have seemed as if a miracle had been repeated for, their benefit.

We made them welcome to our ship, showed them the marvels of our equipment, and treated them with the greatest consideration. They asked if they might not come and bring their tribe and settle near us. To this we agreed, and it was not long before fifty Eskimo huts sprang up about our camp, housing about two hundred men, women, and children.

This was an opportunity to delight the soul of an anthropologist and ethnographer. We had hoped for just such good fortune as this when we planned the expedition, and in consequence had brought many things for the purpose of barter. I set about to acquire a complete set of museum exhibits to illustrate every phase of the life of the Eskimo. Before I finished, I had several such complete sets, which now repose in the Norwegian museums. I got samples of literally everything these Eskimos possessed, from suits of clothing worn by both sexes, young and old, to samples of every kind of implement they had for cooking, sledding, and the chase. Some marvellous bargains were included in this collection. For example, for the price of an empty tin I got two complete sets of women's clothing. To me it was wonderful to see the artistic sense and fabricating skill evidenced in these garments. The women are very adept at cutting out the black parts and the white parts of the caribou skins and fashioning them into beautiful shapes and then working these parts of skins into elaborate patterns. Their bead work, too, made from the teeth and bits of dried bone of the caribou, showed taste and skill.

Imagine, too, the interest I took in the implements used by these people. Their skill in taking the bones of freshly killed game and stretching and twisting them while still green into proper lengths and shapes from which to fashion spear heads and shaft needles for sewing, and other useful articles, was to me a fascinating example of human ingenuity.

Another bargain was the exchange I made of one heavy steel needle for four of the most beautiful white fox skins I have ever seen in all my Arctic experience. Some of these trades may sound like hard bargains on our part, but this was not the case. The Eskimos traded us only of their surplus for things of our stock which to them were of equal value. A hunting knife of fine Swedish steel could easily be worth to an Eskimo hunter far more than a dozen beautiful furs for which he had no present need and which he could easily duplicate.

By this process, during the two years that we remained in this camp, the Eskimos got from us everything we had that was of use to them, and we, in turn, got our complete collection of their products. It was a perfect example of a good bargain, in which both sides profited.

As soon as the Eskimos began settling down around us, I was confronted with a situation which the commander of every expedition has to meet on any exploration which brings white men and savages into contact in the wilds. To all savages, the civilized white man has some of the attributes of the gods. His deadly and mysterious weapons, his devices for producing instant fire and light, his wealth of equipment and variety of food seem to these untutored minds to stamp him with divine origin. This superstitious fear is the strongest safeguard of the explorer.

So long as it persists, one man like myself with six followers would be safe among 200 Eskimos, for example.

But one thing, more surely than anything else, can dissipate this godly elevation. The white man may even be brutal with the savage and still retain his respect, for ruthless power is also in their minds an attribute of divinity. But the moment the white man yields to his baser passions and takes liberties with the savages' women, he falls in their eyes to the level of mere man and puts himself at their mercy. I therefore took the first opportunity to have a most serious talk with my companions and urge them not to yield to this kind of temptation.

When we left, we gave the Eskimos many articles that we no longer needed. In their eyes, the priceless gift we made them was the wood of which our house and observatories were built. They did not possess a stick of their own; and this gift meant to them an abundant supply of materials for the manufacture of sleds, spear handles, and other invaluable articles.

The scientific data we brought home were enormous in quantity. So extended and complete were our magnetic observations that the scientists to whom we delivered them, on our return to Europe in 1906, have spent nearly twenty years in digesting their meaning, having only last year finished their calculations based upon these data. Nothing anywhere nearly so complete regarding the phenomena of the North Magnetic Pole has ever before been given to science. Meanwhile, the rest of the Northwest Passage was still before us. We left our camp on August 13, 1905, and set sail through Simpson Strait. Much of this coast had been mapped by earlier explorers who had travelled to it by land from Hudson Bay, but no vessel had ever heretofore troubled these waters or charted their shallows – they do not deserve the title of "depths." If they had, we should have had an easier time of it. But time and again it seemed certain we should be defeated by the shallowness of these tortuous channels. Day after day, for three weeks – the longest three weeks of my life – we crept along, sounding our depth with the lead, trying here, there, and everywhere to nose into a channel that would carry us clear through to the known waters to the west. Once, in Simpson Strait, we had just an inch of water to spare beneath our keel!

While this final effort for our goal was on, I could not eat or sleep. Food stuck in my throat when I tried to swallow. Every nerve was strained to the limit in the resolve to foresee every danger and to avoid every pitfall. We *must* succeed!

"A sail! A sail!"

We *had* succeeded! What a glorious sight that was – the distant outlines of a whaling vessel in the west! It meant the end of years of hope and toil, for that vessel had come from San Francisco through Bering Strait and along the north coast of Alaska, and where its deep belly had floated, we could float, so that all doubts of our success in making the Northwest Passage were at an end. Victory was ours!

Instantly, my nerve-racking strain of the last three weeks was over. And with its passing, my appetite returned. I felt ravenous. Hanging from the shrouds were carcasses of caribou. I rushed up the rigging, knife in hand. Furiously I slashed off slice after slice of the raw meat, thrusting it down my throat in chunks and ribbons, like a famished animal, until I could contain no more. Appetite demanded, but my stomach rejected, this barbarous feast. I had to "feed the fishes." But my appetite would not be denied, and again I ate my fill of raw, half-frozen meat. This time it stayed by me, and soon I was restored to a sense of calm well-being such as I had not known in the three terrible weeks just passed. Those weeks had left their mark upon me in such a way that my age was guessed to be between fifty-nine and seventy-five years, although I was only thirty-three!

The whaler was the *Charles Hansson,* of San Francisco, and the date we sighted her was August 26, 1905. After a visit with the captain of the whaler, we started on our way to Bering Strait to complete the passage. Little did we imagine that it would take us another year to negotiate this perfectly simple concluding portion of the trip. The ice grew thicker and thicker as we slowly advanced, so that, within a week, on September 2d, we came to a dead stop off King Point on the north coast of Canada.

It was soon clear that we should have to winter at this point. The Arctic night was coming on, and the ice made further progress impossible. We therefore selected the most favourable spot available, behind a grounded ice floe, tied the ship up, and began preparations for another winter in the North. We soon had everything comfortably disposed for the winter. Our progress had been so slow that we were only a few miles from the whaling vessels which, of course, were also iced in for the winter at Herschel Island. We should not lack for company. It soon became apparent, from an undercurrent of talk that came to our ears, that we were not altogether welcome *neighbours.* One of the whaling captains even grumbled that we would be only "seven more mouths to feed." Before the winter was over, he and the rest realized that we were better provisioned than they. We never asked them for any supplies, and, on the contrary, during the winter sent them two tons of wheat flour, of which they had come out short-rationed.

On King Point was beached the whaler *Bonanza,* which had been pushed ashore by the ice during the summer. Her commander shared with me an adventure I shall now relate. He was extremely anxious to get back overland to San Francisco, so that he could outfit another vessel and be ready to come up again to the North the following spring – otherwise, he would lose one whole whaling season.

On my part, I was wild with eagerness to get to a telegraph office and send the news to the world of our success in conquering the Northwest Passage. The nearest telegraph office was five hundred miles away on the far side of a range of mountains 9,000 feet high, which we should have to traverse in the season of short days. Nevertheless, so eager were we both that we resolved to make the journey.

I had no fears of the journey itself, but I had considerable apprehensions of making it with Captain Mogg of the *Bonanza*. First of all, he had the money and I had none, so he would be in command of our little party. In the nature of things, I was sure that he was far less competent for this kind of an expedition than I. In the second place, Captain Mogg was short and fat, so that there was no possibility that he could run with the sledges; but rather the certainty that he would have to ride on one of them and be dragged by one dog team.

Nevertheless, I was too anxious to make the trip to decline the opportunity, even with these handicaps. But my heart sank when we began discussing provisions for the journey. I had on the *Gjoa* a number of cases of pemmican in tin – the ideal provision for any long journey over the snow, because pemmican, being dried meat and fat in equal portions, is the most condensed form of satisfactory nourishment in a cold climate that has ever been devised. But when I proposed to Captain Mogg that we take these tins as our chief provision, he scornfully and positively refused, asserting that such food was not fit for a dog to eat. The alternative which he proposed, and which perforce I had to accept, was numerous sacks of cooked and frozen beans! To say nothing of their infinitely less nutritive value in proportion to their bulk, even the most unskilled dweller in the Temperate Zone can imagine how much needless waste of water content in the beans we should be dragging over the weary miles of snow. However, there was nothing to do about it, and thus provisioned we set forth from Herschel Island on October 24, 1905.

We had two sledges and twelve dogs, the property of our Eskimo guide Jim. His wife Kappa made the fourth member of our little expedition.

Our course ran up Herschel Island River, over the mountain summit of 9,000 feet elevation, and down the southern slopes to the Yukon River, where we encountered the first trading post at Fort Yukon.

Jim ran ahead of one team to break the snow, and I ahead of the other. Physically, I was not very hard when we started, after our many weeks on the *Gjoa*, but in a few days I got my second wind, and we readily made twenty-five to thirty miles a day through the heavy snow. This was not so bad, but the scantiness of the food at night told heavily on all of us but Captain Mogg. He, of course, did no work during the day, as he simply sat on one of the sleds. To the other three of us, however, our little ration of a handful of cooked beans was wholly inadequate to replace the drain on our muscles from the exertions of the day. We grew hungrier and thinner with every mile.

We left Jim and Kappa at Fort Yukon, and Captain Mogg and I set forth down the Yukon with one team, the Captain still riding and I still running in the lead. From this point on, our journey held no dangers because the roadhouses are situated, by intention, just half a day's travel apart, and, of course, the frozen river bed showed us the way. Captain Mogg, however, was so anxious to get as quickly as possible to civilization that he insisted we should not stop for lunch but should make an unbroken run from breakfast to dinner. I protested strongly against this scheme, reminding him of the difference in the exertions which he and I were making and of my greater need for food. The Captain angrily dismissed my protest and pointed out that, as he was the commander of the expedition, and, what was more important, had all the money, his orders would prevail. I said nothing, but, like the Irishman's parrot, "I kept up a devil of a thinking." The next morning we started from the roadhouse in the bright sunshine through deep snow. I led the way on the run until we were exactly halfway between the roadhouse we had left and the one we should reach at noon. There I stopped the dogs and told Captain Mogg that, from this point, he could proceed alone – I would return on foot to the roadhouse we had left behind. The team of dogs, the sled, and all the supplies belonged to him, and, of course, I would leave them with him. There was no reason why he should not go on ahead by himself.

The Captain was dumbfounded and was also frightened almost to death. He piteously exclaimed that I was leaving him to perish in the wilderness, as he knew nothing of the management of the dogs and was physically unequal to walking, to say nothing of the fact that he was wholly inexperienced in Northern travel. "True enough," I replied, "but that is your responsibility. I am not able to go on with this journey without three meals a day, and all three of them adequate to my bodily needs. The only condition on which I will go a foot farther is that you will agree to feed me properly."

The Captain could not give his assent quickly enough to assuage his fears that I might change even this simple condition and leave him to his fate. Then, having his assurance that I should be properly fed three times a day, we proceeded on our course. We arrived at Fort Egbert on December 5, 1905. I remember that the thermometer was sixty degrees below zero. Fort Egbert was the northernmost post of the United States army and at the end of the army telegraph line. I was greeted with flattering enthusiasm by the commander at the post, who overpowered me with congratulations and with invitations to make a protracted stay as his guest. I did not feel that I could do this, but I did accept with deep gratitude his offer to send out my telegrams. I wrote out about a thousand words which were at once put on the wire. By an odd freak of circumstance, they had no sooner been sent than the cold somewhere on the line broke the wires, and it was not until a week later that they were repaired and I received confirmation that my telegram had reached the outer world. Of course, I received many telegrams and cables of congratulation and exchanged business messages with my brother in Oslo, who managed my affairs.

During this week of waiting and the subsequent weeks of recuperation I was the guest of Mr Frank N. Smith, the resident manager of the Alaska Commercial Company, to whom I shall ever be grateful for his hospitality.

I left Fort Egbert in February of 1906 and made my way back past the chain of trading stations to rejoin Jim and Kappa, with whom I set out on the return trip to the *Gjoa*. This time we took care to get more sensible and more adequate provisions, so that to us three, all accustomed to travel in the Arctic, the return journey was a picnic.

One morning, soon after we had reached Porcupine River going north, Jim gave an exclamation of surprise and pointed to the distance ahead. His keen eyes had discovered a black spot moving on the snow. Soon I, too, could discern it. Another hour and we came up to a solitary man, his face black with smoke, accompanied not even by a dog, and dragging his toboggan behind him. This was Mr Darrell, the mail carrier, taking mail from the mouth of the Mackenzie River over to the trading posts on the other side of the mountains. I could not believe my eyes. Here was a man, hundreds of miles from the nearest human being, with not a soul to aid him in case of illness or accident, cheerfully trudging through the Arctic winter across an unblazed wilderness, and thinking nothing at all of his exploit.

I was lost in admiration of this hearty and cheerful Scotsman. We became warm friends at once, and subsequently he wrote me many letters, in the last of which he asked me to include him in my impending expedition to the South Pole. I was delighted at the opportunity to get him, and he would certainly have been a member of that expedition had not fate intervened. He was lost at the mouth of the Mackenzie River and never heard from again. I cannot forbear taking this opportunity to pay tribute to the memory of one of the finest men of the Northern breed that it has ever been my good fortune to meet.

Otherwise, our trip back to Herschel Island was without incident. The ice broke up in July, and without much difficulty we made our way to Point Barrow. Thence we passed through Bering Strait and on down the coast to San Francisco, which we reached in the month of October. Here I made the city a present of the *Gjoa* as a historical souvenir of our conquest of the Northwest Passage. She still reposes in the Golden Gate Park at San Francisco, under an appropriate shelter, for observation by the curious.

I should not conclude this chapter without a brief glance at the history of preceding attempts to navigate the Northwest Passage. Before I had started on that adventure, I had the good fortune in 1899 to buy all the literature upon the Northwest Passage from an old gentleman in Grimsby, England. By reading these books, I had thoroughly informed myself in the literature of this specialty before I made my successful attempt. A glance at the North Polar map will show that there appeared to be numberless possible channels threading the maze of islands off the north coast of North America. Superficially, it would appear that the obvious route would be almost due westerly from the north end of Boothia Felix, where the map gives the appearance of fairly open waters clear across. This indeed was the route which most previous explorers had attempted, with uniform lack of success. The distinctive characteristic of my successful venture was that I turned south along the west coast of Boothia Felix to the southernmost point of King William Island, and then proceeded on my way westward, closely following the coast. I owe a good part of my success to the old gentleman in Grimsby, for it was in one of those books, Admiral Sir Leopold McClintock's account of his search for Sir John Franklin, that I read a prophecy that the true channel would be found by following a more southerly route than that taken by previous explorers. It was largely due to this prophecy that I adopted that route.

Many of the earlier attempts to conquer the Northwest Passage were made by expeditions sent out by the British government in attempts to rescue Sir John Franklin, who had never come back from his last expedition. He and his men had perished from starvation – oddly enough, at a spot where, when we reached it, we happened to find an abundance of game on land and fish in the water.

Some years before, the British government had offered a standing prize of $100,000 to the first discoverer of the passage. This prize was divided between Dr John Rae of the Hudson's Bay Company and Admiral Sir Robert Le Messurier McClure. My successful voyage in the *Gjoa* was the first *navigation of* the Northwest Passage, and remains to this day the only navigation of it. Indeed, it is most unlikely that anyone in the future will think it worth while to consider it for a second, in view of the fact that there are so many great difficulties and dangers involved.

The basis on which the British government awarded the prize to Dr John Rae and Admiral Sir Robert McClure was this:

Sir Robert had attempted the passage from the west and had proceeded as far as the Bay of Mercy on Banks Land. Here he had to abandon his ship, and he and his expedition were ultimately brought back to civilization by a rescue party that came to Banks Land from the east.

Dr John Rae was an officer of the Hudson's Bay Company. He never attempted the navigation of the passage at all, but, as leader of several overland expeditions to the north coast of Canada, made most valuable maps and gave the first sure proofs of the fate of the Franklin expedition.

Needless to say, however much these able men deserved remuneratory rewards for their hardships and achievements, the voyage of the *Gjoa* stands as the first and only actual navigation of the Northwest Passage.

Having achieved the first ambition of my life, I began looking about for new worlds to conquer. I devoted 1906 and 1907 to lecturing in Europe and the United States, and returned to Norway with enough funds to repay all my creditors, including the one who had nearly prevented the voyage, and I was now free to make other plans.

CHAPTER IV

The Dash To The South Pole

The next exploit which I resolved to attempt was the capture of the North Pole. I was anxious to try on my own account the venture Dr Nansen had made some years before, of drifting on the Polar currents across the North Pole and clear on across the Arctic Sea. For this purpose, I secured Dr Nansen's famous ship *Fram*, and though she was now a good deal the worse for age and wear, I felt she was still capable of standing the pounding of the Polar ice and would carry an expedition safely. I made all my plans, reconditioned the *Fram*, provisioned her, and had chosen my companions, even an aviator, for the attempt. Then, just as everything was about ready, the world was electrified by the news that Admiral Peary, in April, 1909, had reached the North Pole. This was a blow indeed! If I was to maintain my prestige as an explorer, I must quickly achieve a sensational success of some sort. I resolved upon a coup, announcing that I still felt the scientific value of such a journey justified the effort. I left Norway in August, 1910, with my companions.

Our plan for the drift provided that we should enter the Arctic Ocean through Bering Strait, as we believed the main drift was in that direction. Our route from Norway to Bering Strait was by way of Cape Horn. First we touched the Madeira Islands. Here I informed my crew that I – as the North Pole had been discovered – had decided to go for the South Pole. All agreed enthusiastically.

The story of our success on this expedition has been fully told in my book, *The South Pole*, which has been published in two editions in English. The story of Captain Scott's expedition has also been so widely read that it would be merely a repetition to cover the ground again in this place. I t is, however, worth while to make some observations on the reasons for our safe return from that hazardous adventure and for the tragic death of Captain Scott and his companions. I wish also at this point frankly to meet some criticisms of my action in competing with Captain Scott, which are based on popular misapprehension of some essential facts and which, I feel, has left me unfairly compromised in many minds. One story is to the effect that, from a sporting point of view, I took an unfair advantage of Captain Scott in that I gave him no notice, so the story goes, of my intention to make my expedition a race with his. The truth is quite otherwise.

Captain Scott had the fullest possible notice of my intentions, both before he left Australia and again after we had both established our base camps in the Antarctic. When I sailed from Madeira in the fall of 1910, I left with my secretary a sealed envelope containing a cablegram to Captain Scott in Australia, which he, in accordance with my instructions, sent a few days after we were safe at sea, and which disclosed fully my intention to compete with Captain Scott for the South Pole.

Later, in the winter (which, of course, was the summer in the Antarctic), a party from the Scott expedition came to our camp in the Bay of Whales – about four hundred miles from Scott's camp – and saw all our preparations there. Both parties necessarily had to spend the winter in camp to await the earliest practicable weather to attempt the dash to the Pole. Not only did we extend to these men every hospitality and the opportunity to inspect our equipment, but I also invited them to stay with us and make use of half of our dogs. They refused. All my experience in Polar work had convinced me that dogs were the only practicable draught animals for use in snow and ice. They are quick, strong, sure-footed, intelligent, and able to negotiate any terrain that man himself can traverse. Scott, on the other hand, had come South equipped with motor sledges, which had immediately demonstrated their impracticability over the surface of ice and snow. He had brought also – and to these he pinned his fate finally – a number of Shetland ponies. I was confident that this was a fatal mistake, and much to my sorrow it was in part the cause of Scott's tragic end.

So, I repeat, I had decisively given him ample notice before he made his attempt.

Our choice of a site for our base camp on the barrier was an essential factor in our success, just as Scott's choice of a site on the mainland to the west was an essential factor in his inability to return in safety from the Pole. In the first place, the air currents in the Antarctic regions make the weather much more severe on the land than on the ice. At best the climate in the Antarctic is about the worst in the world, chiefly because of the terrific intensity of the gales which blow almost incessantly in those regions. These gales are of almost unbelievable velocity. Scott encountered them several times of such force that it was nearly impossible to stand erect. In his winter camp, Scott and his companions were harassed through the weary waiting months with almost uninterrupted bad weather – something which not only lowered the spirits of the party but also seriously hampered their work of preparation for the final dash. Our camp on the ice, however, was favoured with infinitely better weather, and at no time were we subject to any discomfort. Our experience of the past in preparing an absolutely windproof shelter, and in solving the problem of ventilating such a shelter, provided us with fairly comfortable winter quarters.

The ice barrier – so much described in all works on Antarctic exploration – is in reality nothing but a gigantic glacier pressing down from the heights of the Antarctic mountains to the sea. This glacier is hundreds of miles in width and from one to two hundred feet high. Like all glaciers, at its lower end this one was constantly breaking off into icebergs. The idea, therefore, of making a permanent camp on the barrier itself, though often considered, had always been dismissed as too dangerous.

I had, however, carefully read and long pondered the works of the earlier explorers in the Antarctic. In comparing their records, I had been greatly struck with the discovery that the Bay of Whales, notwithstanding that it was merely a bay whose shores were the icy walls of the glacier, had not substantially changed its shore line since its first discovery by Sir James Ross in 1842. "Surely," I said to myself, "if this part of the glacier has not moved in sixty-eight years, there can be only one explanation of the phenomenon-the glacier at this point must be firmly wedged upon the solid rock of some great and immovable island." The more I thought of this explanation, the more I became convinced of its truth. I had, therefore, no fear of the stability of our camp site when I resolved to make our permanent land quarters on the top of the barrier in the Bay of Whales. Needless to add, my faith was entirely justified by subsequent events. We had the most delicate instruments and we made continuous observations for months, none of which disclosed the slightest movement of the barrier of ice at this point.

Our location on the Bay of Whales gave us several advantages in trying to reach the Pole. In the first place, it was somewhat nearer to the Pole than Scott's camp, and, as the event proved, the path southward which it forced us to take was much the more favourable for travel.

Above all of these things, however, the one which was most essential to our success was our use of dogs. The reason briefly is this: Our method of attacking the Pole was to make repeated trips from the permanent camp southward, setting up shelters and making caches of provisions one after the other at several days' travel apart, so that we should be able to make the return trip from the Pole without having to carry all our supplies there and back. Obviously, we could set up this series of caches very quickly, and at each we could safely leave the minimum weight of supplies for the return trip. In making my calculations for the distances between these stations and the amount of provisions which should be left in each, I was able to reduce the weight of provisions to be carried by calculating the flesh of the dogs which carried it as part of the food supply of us men. As there are about fifty pounds of edible food in the carcass of an Eskimo dog, it was quite probable that every dog we took south with us meant fifty less pounds of food to be carried and cached. In my calculations before the start for the final dash to the Pole, I figured out exactly the precise day on which I planned to kill each dog as its usefulness should end for drawing the diminishing supplies on the sleds and its usefulness should begin as food for the men. This schedule worked out almost to the day and the dog. Above everything else, it was the essential factor in our successful trip to the Pole and our safe return to the base camp.

Scott and his companions died on their return from the Pole, not from broken hearts over our earlier arrival, but from actual starvation, because of their inability to provide adequately for food on the return trip. This difference between the two expeditions was exactly the difference between dogs and other means of transportation.

The rest of what happened is a familiar story. With four companions, I reached the South Pole in December, 1911, camped there for three days, and then explored the neighbourhood of our camp within a radius of ten miles so as to make sure, if our observations were slightly in error, that we should, nevertheless, set foot on the actual site of the Pole. We left the Norwegian flag and the records of our observations in a tent at the Pole and returned safely to our camp. A month later, in January, 1912, Scott arrived at the Pole and found these records. Scott and his four companions made a gallant effort to return to their base camp, but perished of starvation and exposure before they could reach it.

Nobody could hold a higher admiration than myself for the gallant courage of our brave English competitors, for nobody else so well as we can understand the fearful dangers of the trip.

Scott was a splendid sportsman as well as a great explorer. I cannot, however, say as much for many of his countrymen. Just as in times of war it may be observed that the soldiers on the opposing sides retain a high respect for their foes in arms, while the noncombatants at home seem to feel obligated to indulge in hymns of hate against their enemies, just so in exploration it often happens that the men in the field retain a high regard for their competitors, while their effortless compatriots at home seem to feel obligated to detract from the success of an explorer just because he is not of their own nation. Meaning that the following comment shall be read in the light of the preceding sentence, I feel justified in saying that by and large the British are a race of very bad losers. I have felt the effects of this trait in many a way in relation to our capture of both the Northwest Passage and the South Pole, of which a couple of examples will suffice to illustrate my meaning.

The year following the capture of the Pole, the son of a prominent Norwegian in London came home from his classes at an English school one evening, protesting to his father that he was being taught that Scott was the discoverer of the South Pole. On investigation, the boy's protest was found to be a fact, and the practice of ignoring the Norwegian success was being followed in other schools as well.

But a more flagrant and offensive incident, because it came from a quarter better informed and less justified in equivocation, occurred at the dinner tendered me in London by the Royal Geographical Society, presided over by the nominal president of the Society, Lord Curzon of Kedleston. At this banquet Lord Curzon made a speech. After describing in appropriate detail the reason for my lecture and laying some stress upon the value which I had attached to the dogs as contributors to our success, Lord Curzon ended his speech with the phrase, "I therefore propose three cheers for the dogs" clearly indicating the next moment the satirical and derogatory intention of the phrase by turning to me with an unnecessary calming gesture and, though I had made no move, urging me with great earnestness not to make a rejoinder to the thinly veiled insult. Our first stop on our way back to Europe in the *Fram* was at Buenos Aires. At this point, I must not fail to record my undying gratitude to Mr Pedro Christophersen, a wealthy Norwegian, who made his home in the capital city of the Argentine. His timely aid with funds, sound advice, and personal good offices more than once saved the expedition from failure.

We were received in Europe with many honours, not only in my native land but in other countries. And upon my visit shortly after to the United States, I was treated with flattering kindness. The National Geographic Society gave me the large gold medal of the Society, which I received in Washington in the presence of a distinguished company. I shall never cease to regret, therefore, that some incident of this visit apparently put me in the bad graces of this Society, which has ever since taken many opportunities to treat me with a bewildering lack of consideration-. I say "bewildering" because I was unable at that time, and have never since been able, to learn what was the cause of my falling into disfavour with them.

There were also later inconsiderate acts of the National Geographic Society toward me. The most painful of these happened in the spring of 1926. I was lecturing in the United States on the successful Amundsen-Ellsworth flight by 'planes into the heart of the Arctic at 88° N. latitude. I had received and accepted an invitation to make an address on this subject before the National Geographic Society in Washington, D. C., upon the conclusion of this tour. My itinerary eastward from the Pacific coast took me through Kansas City and within a short distance of the Federal penitentiary at Fort Leavenworth. Recalling my acquaintanceship with Dr Cook during our two hazardous years on the *Belgica* expedition to the Antarctic, remembering also the debt of gratitude I owed him for his kindness to me in my novitiate as an explorer, and recalling that I owed my life indeed to his resourcefulness in extricating us from the dangers of that expedition, I felt I could do no less than to make the short journey to the prison and call upon my former benefactor in his present misfortune. I could not have done less without convicting myself of base ingratitude and contemptible cowardice. I did not then, nor will I now, discuss the career of Dr Cook in his later days. I am wholly unfamiliar with the facts which led to his imprisonment, and I have no desire to know them or to have an opinion regarding them. Even had I known that he had been guilty of baser crimes than those with which he was charged, I would still have felt my duty and my inclination to be the same. Whatever Cook may have done, the Cook who did them was not the Dr Cook I knew as a young man, the soul of honour and kindliness, lion-hearted in courage. Some physical misfortune must have overtaken him to change his personality, for which he was not responsible.

The reporters who talked to me after this visit to Dr Cook broadcast a story in which they quoted me as intimating that Peary's proofs that he had reached the Pole were not conclusive, and that Cook's proofs that he had reached the Pole were. The truth is that I did not even discuss this subject with any newspaper man and that these quotations ascribed to me were pure fabrications. The National Geographic Society, however, accepted them as bona fide, declined to accept my telegraphic protest that I had been utterly misquoted, and abruptly cancelled their invitation to address them.

Doubtless, they felt justified in taking this drastic action in view of their belief in the newspaper reports. Needless to say, I felt that they acted with inconsiderate precipitateness, and of course I know they acted upon misapprehension of the facts.

Returning now to 1914: The *Fram* was navigated to Norway while I was in Norway arranging to provision and outfit her for the attempt to drift across the Pole. I had proceeded so far as to buy a Farman biplane to be carried on the *Fram* on this drifting expedition, for use in making explorations of the Arctic ice fields from the air. This was the second time I had set about to use aircraft for Arctic exploration, and it is important to remember this fact and the date 1914, because of their bearing upon my expeditions of 1925 and 1926 over the Arctic by airplane and dirigible. Their significance will appear in a later chapter.

The Farman had been delivered to me at Oslo when the World War broke loose in all its fury. This catastrophe, of course, put all interest in Arctic exploration out of the public mind. I therefore presented the biplane to the Norwegian government for use as part of the defence equipment of the Norwegian army.

CHAPTER V

In The Grip Of
The Northern Ice Pack

During the war, I had nothing else to do, so I decided to emulate the example of so many other citizens in all the neutral countries and try to make a fortune. I hoped to amass enough funds to outfit my next expedition myself. No one but a penniless explorer can realize the frightful handicap from which nearly all explorers suffer in having to waste time and nervous energy in their efforts to raise the money to equip their expeditions. The heartbreaking discouragements, the endless delays, the blows to pride, if not to self-respect, involved in this search for funds, are a tragedy of the explorer's life. I now thought I saw an opportunity for once to avoid these sorrows.

Such an opportunity was obvious in all the neutral countries, and nowhere more obvious than in Norway. Ships were vital to the success of the Allies, and Norway's excellent merchant fleet commanded prodigious prices for its services. I invested all my small capital in shipping, and, like many others, prospered handsomely. Not being in business for any love of business, I withdrew from these enterprises in 1916, when I thought I had enough. By that time I had amassed about one million kroner, which at the value of money then was equivalent to about two hundred and fifty thousand American dollars. This would be adequate to pay for an entirely new and complete expedition, such as I planned for drifting across the Arctic Ocean.

Now that I could afford something better, I was no longer content to use the *Fram*. She was old, her timbers clearly showed signs of decay, and she would need most extensive overhauling to prepare her for the journey. Besides this, I had designed a boat far better for my purpose. This design I submitted to a competent naval architect and shipbuilder, Christian Jensen, who prepared working drawings and agreed to build it. They called for a vessel 120 feet long, 40 feet beam. But the shape of her hull was of much more importance. This was to be the same shape substantially as the half of an egg cut through its length. In other words, the vessel's bottom would be rounded at every point, so that, when she should be caught in the grinding ice, there would be no surface on which the ice could take hold, while, on the contrary, the ice pressure would tend only to lift her to the surface. This shape also provided the greatest strength with the least surface.

I was not satisfied to use the timbers available in Norway, so I imported specially fine timbers from Holland. This involved extraordinary expense both for the material itself and for freight to Norway. The vessel was constructed in a shipyard near Oslo. She was successfully launched on June 7, 1917, and was christened the *Maud* in honour of our beloved queen.

My next task was to load the vessel with provisions and supplies for the journey. These I purchased in the United States, buying my bacon, for example, from Armour's in Chicago, and the other supplies from Sprague, Warner & Company, Chicago. While these preparations were proceeding, I was invited by the United States government to visit the battle fronts in France and Belgium. Probably the occasion of this invitation was the following incident:

In October, 1917, the Germans had begun their ruthless methods of carrying on submarine warfare. I did not then, nor do I yet, see any reason to criticize the Germans for using their submarines to destroy enemy shipping, or even neutral shipping where there was reasonable evidence that it was engaged in carrying contraband of war. Germany's only hope of victory lay in preventing the Allies from receiving essential supplies by water. The use of submarines for this purpose seems to me quite legitimate. Never, however, could I admit their right to use submarines for this purpose except after search of the offending vessel and the removal of passengers and crew to safety. Therefore, when the Germans threw humanity overboard and proceeded to indiscriminate sinkings without warning, I shared the hot indignation of all civilized people.

Naturally, my indignation boiled over in October, 1917, when a German submarine sank a Norwegian merchant vessel in the North Sea without warning, destroying all those on board, and even firing on such lifeboats as could be launched in the confusion.

The Kaiser, personally, before the war had pinned one of my German decorations on my coat in honour of my success at the South Pole. I had, besides, other German decorations.

The day we received word in Norway of this brutal sinking of one of our merchant ships, I was powerfully impelled to make an emphatic demonstration of my indignation. My habit of self-control withheld me from acting upon impulse. I allowed myself twenty-four hours to deliberate upon my first emotion. When the twenty-four hours were up, I had not changed my mind. It was therefore with perfect deliberation and reasoned intention that I made my way to the German Legation in Oslo. In my pocket was an envelope containing all my German decorations and medals and a formal letter that I had written. At the Legation, I was ushered into the presence of the Prince of Wied, who was acting German Minister. I had met him socially on numerous occasions, and our relations had always been pleasant. Naturally, he came forward with a smile and outstretched hand to greet me. I had no smile for him and I ignored his hand. I announced that I had come on a matter of serious business, and for fear that I should not speak impromptu with force enough to express my feelings, I read my carefully written letter to him. In this I expressed my indignation and resentment, and declared that I had brought with me, to be returned to the Emperor, the medals and decorations he had conferred upon me, which, now that I viewed the donor with abhorrence and contempt, I no longer valued.

The United States government probably heard of this incident, and partly as a result of it extended me the invitation mentioned above. Through the invitation, I visited Admiral Sims in London in January, 1918, where he generously explained all the details of the Allied naval plans for control of the submarine menace.

In the spring of 1918, I lectured in the United States upon my experience at the front and returned to Norway only a couple of weeks before the *Maud* was ready to start on her long voyage. I had now decided to get into the Arctic by the shortest possible route. I therefore planned to skirt the coast of Norway from Oslo to Tromsoe. Thence I should make the Northeast Passage along the north coast of Europe and Asia, passing Cape Tscheluskin and rounding the New Siberian Islands, when I could strike into the same Arctic current which I would have made by proceeding first to Bering Strait.

Shortly before the *Maud* was due to sail from Oslo, in the late spring of 1918, the Norwegian Minister at Berlin wrote to me advising me that it would be wise to procure the consent of the German naval authorities to my passage through the Arctic Sea; otherwise, the submarines might torpedo the *Maud*. I declared that I would never ask this favour of any government.

Here again the kindness of Admiral Sims was most useful to me. Through intelligence sent by him, I was advised of a favourable time to proceed – when all the German submarines operating in the Arctic Sea had returned to their base for supplies. We left Tromsoe on July 15, 1918, and headed eastward along the north coast of Europe.

The following ten days, however, were tense with apprehension to all on board, because we knew that, until we had passed the White Sea, we could not be sure that some stray submarine might not be cruising in the waters there. Our apprehension gave rise to an amusing incident on July 25th, when we reached Yugor Strait. Only the watch was on deck, and all the rest were below. A sudden storm made it necessary to call all hands aloft to help handle the ship, so I suddenly appeared at the companionway and shouted down, "All hands on deck. Quick!" A few moments later, I was bewildered when I saw the crew tumbling up the companionway. Some of the boys appeared in the scantiest of night apparel, some with pieces of other men's clothing pulled on awry, and one in a complete suit of civilian street clothes, bowler hat and all, with his suitcase in his hand. The bewilderment gave way to mirth when I realized that my abrupt call to the deck had been interpreted as a warning that we were about to be torpedoed by a submarine. My laughter and a look at the weather told the boys of their mistake, and, of course, they soon reappeared equipped for sea duty.

The Northeast Passage had, of course, been navigated before our expedition, and it offers no great difficulties to experienced navigators. The first place we had any trouble worth mentioning was in the Kara Sea, but this was rather easily overcome. On September 1st we arrived at Dickson Island, where we took on a supply of gasoline and departed eastward four days later. On September 9th, we passed Cape Tscheluskin, noteworthy only as being the northernmost point of Asia. We were now encountering heavy ice and could make slow progress only along a narrow lane near shore.

By September 13th, the ice became quite impassable. We therefore began looking about for a place to tie up for the winter.

The site was most unfavourable for our purposes. No such landlocked harbour as had favoured us on the Northwest Passage was at hand, nor indeed a harbour of any sort. The only hope of shelter lay behind two tiny islets, which might in some degree lessen the impact of the ice pressing toward the shore from the north. It was easy work to reach the coast here, as an open channel led right in behind the islets to the beach, but inviting as it looked, I feared it might act as a kind of a rat trap to us.

We made the lee of the islets and tied up to the land ice two hundred yards from the beach. We named this rather uncertain haven Maud Harbour, and in spite of its unfavourable first aspect, it sheltered us safely for a year.

As soon as we had tied up, we went ashore to find out if the beach was fitted for our different observatories, kennels, etc. We found this to be the case, and built our observatories, and kennels for twenty dogs. We made quick work of our preparations, so that, within three weeks, or on September 30th, everything was finished and we were in comfortable shape for the winter.

The searching Arctic winds are the greatest handicap to comfort in winter quarters, so our next enterprise was to shovel snow against the sides of the *Maud* until we had piled up a snowbank all around her nearly to the deck level and sloping steeply downward to the level of the ice. For convenience we made a gangplank at an easier grade, in such a manner as to make a runway leading from the ice up to the deck of the *Maud* at the point nearest to the door to the cabin. One side of this runway was provided with a rope hand rail to which, in slippery weather, one could cling to keep from falling.

One of the dogs was a female who was expecting shortly to have a litter. She was very fond of me, and every morning when I came out of the cabin she would come running to me to be petted. I would pick her up in my arms and carry her down the runway to the ice so that she could accompany me on the morning walk which I took to keep in good condition. One morning, when I had got her in my arms and was just about to start down the runway, Jacob, the watchdog of the *Maud,* came running toward me and bumped against me so that my feet went out from under me and I plunged headlong down the steep slope at the side of the runway, landing on my right shoulder with the weight of my whole body on top of it. For a few moments I saw stars. When I came to, I managed to sit up on the ice, but found that my shoulder was giving me excruciating pain. I had no doubt it was a bad fracture, as X-rays three years later proved was the case. I succeeded in climbing aboard again and into my cabin. Here Wisting, who had studied first aid at a hospital in Oslo, did his best to get the fracture set. The pain was so intense and the swelling so bad that neither he nor I could tell at the time whether he had succeeded. I was so entirely knocked out by the shock that I kept my bed for eight days. Then I got Wisting to put my arm in a sling and started going about again. But my bad luck was not yet through with me.

On November 8th, I came up on deck so early in the morning that it was still almost as dark as night. A fog added to the gloom. Jacob, the watchdog, came running to me, and after leaping about me in demonstrative fashion for some moments, dashed down the runway and disappeared off on the ice. I did not venture to follow him for fear of another fall, so made my way down the gangway and proceeded alongside the ship, watching carefully to avoid the ice and snow pieces that littered this passage. I had stood below the bow for only a moment when I heard a faint sound so odd that I pricked up my ears to listen better. It seemed like the first faint soughing of the wind in the rigging when a breeze springs up. In a moment it grew louder and was clearly the sound of heavy breathing. Straining my eyes in the direction from which it came, I finally discerned Jacob headed for the ship at the best pace he could muster, and the next instant I saw behind him the huge form of a Polar bear in hot pursuit. It was the breathing of this bear approaching rapidly that I had heard.

Instantly I realized the situation. This was a mother bear with her cub. Jacob had found them and teased the cub. The mother's fury had quickly decided Jacob that he had urgent business on board the ship. The situation had its humorous side, but I did not pause to enjoy that, because I saw it also had its dangers for me. When the bear saw me she sat down and gazed at me. I certainly did the same at her. However, I think our feelings were different. We were both at about the same distance from the gangway. What should I do? I was alone – no assistance – only one arm – the left. Well, I had not much choice. I started to run as quickly as possible for the gangplank, but the bear did the same thing. Now started a race between a healthy, furious bear and an invalid. Not much chance for the latter. As soon as I reached the gangway and turned to run on board, the bear stretched me to the ground with a well-aimed blow on my back. I fell on my broken arm – face down – and expected to be finished right away. But no – my lucky star had not stopped shining yet. Jacob, who had been on board all this time, took suddenly into his head to return – probably to play with the cub. In doing so, he had to pass where mother bear was busy with me. When she saw Jacob passing, she jumped high in the air and left me for Jacob. It did not take me long to get up and disappear into safety. It was one of the narrowest escapes of my life.

This escape has ever since held a curious interest to me because of my psychology at the moment of greatest danger. I had always heard that when a man faced the seeming certainty of death – as for a moment I did, lying at the feet of the bear – he usually had the mental experience of having all the chief incidents of his life pass before him in vivid and instant review. Nothing so serious or important occupied my thoughts as I lay expecting the death blow. On the contrary, a scene passed before my eyes which, though vivid enough, was certainly frivolous. I lay there wondering how many hairpins were swept up on the sidewalks of Regent Street in London on a Monday morning! The significance of this foolish thought at one of the most serious moments of my life I shall have to leave to a psychologist, but I have never ceased to be interested in this personal experience of the strange possibilities of the human mind under stress.

The gashes in my back were of no importance, but I feared the fall had broken my shoulder again, but that was not the case. I now set about a long and painful process of self-cure. At first I could not lift my right hand high enough to use a pencil. Several times a day, therefore, I would sit in a chair, brace my body, grasp my right fist in my left hand, and with the strength of my left arm force my right arm slowly upward a short distance, repeating the painful operation time after time. At the end of the year, I could reach my face, but it took me several months' hard work to get my arm fully strengthened again. The first surgeon I reached was in Seattle in 1921. He took several X-rays, and he and a consultant not only studied them but made a careful physical examination besides. They were greatly astonished at what they found. They told me that my shoulder in the X-rays appeared to be in a condition which theoretically would make it impossible for me to use my arm at all. Thus, among such distinctions as I possess must be counted also the one that I am an impossible but successful surgical phenomenon.

An even more dangerous experience befell me shortly afterward. Our observatory was a very small room with no windows, so that there was very little ventilation. It was both lighted and heated by a patented Swedish lamp in which kerosene, by means of a hand air pump, was transformed into vapour. This vapour was burned at the jet and gave a very beautiful and very hot yellow light. I have used these lamps on all my expeditions, and they are ideal for Arctic work.

One day, I went into the observatory to take observations. After a while, I began to realize that I was a little drowsy and then that my heart was beating unnaturally. At first I realized this only vaguely, as one does not notice slight changes in the surroundings when he is absorbed in work. By the time I became fully aware of my sensations and aroused to my danger, I was on the verge of unconsciousness. By good fortune, I managed to struggle to the door and get out into the fresh air.

I have never been sure exactly what happened whether the flame merely exhausted most of the oxygen in the air, or whether the mixture of the vapour was not right and the lamp was throwing off poisonous fumes. In any event, my system was thoroughly impregnated with the poison and my heart seriously affected. It was several days before the violent palpitation ceased. It was months before I could take any strenuous exercise without feeling my heart pounding, and years before I fully recovered from the effects. Indeed, in 1922, the doctors advised me that I must abandon exploration if I expected to live. Notwithstanding this opinion, I have kept right on with it ever since, and would to-day, at fifty-five years of age, cheerfully wager that I could outrun most young men of twenty-five.

This experience happened about New Year's, and in February I was still so weak that the exercise of climbing a fifty-foot hill near the *Maud* to "see the sun come back" pretty nearly finished me with exhaustion.

Though spring now followed, we were still surrounded by the ice, which did not break up as is usual. Summer came, and still we were locked in behind the islets. There was clear water beyond them, but the problem was to pass the intervening thousand yards or so through the thick masses of land ice. Remembering Dr Cook's expedient on the *Belgica* expedition, we bored fifty holes in the ice in a line leading to free water, and in each hole deposited a charge of explosive, connecting all to a single line of electric wires. We exploded all these charges simultaneously. To our chagrin apparently nothing happened. Nevertheless, I felt sure that the charges must have cracked the ice, even though we could not see the cracks. Studying our navigation books, I found that high tide was to be expected on the night of September 12th. My hope was that the exceptional swell on this evening would so lift the ice that the invisible cracks would be opened and the seemingly unbroken sheet broken up into separate cakes.

I shall never forget that night of September 12th. It was one of the most beautiful scenes I have ever witnessed in my years in the Polar regions. The sky was perfectly clear, and a glorious moon made the whole landscape glisten with a vivid whiteness. In several places we could see Polar bears moving about on the ice. Added to the moonlight was a brilliant display of the aurora.

We stood on deck delighted with the beauty of the night, and yet nervously on edge at the uncertain issue of our hopes about the tide. At last, however, a crackling sound began to issue from the path we had marked with our explosives, and sure enough, soon great cracks appeared and the solid surface was broken into pieces. We wasted no time, but made our way swiftly to open water.

From our departure from this winter camp dates the one real tragedy in all my Polar work. The crew of the *Maud* comprised ten men from Norway. One of the boys suffered from constant headache and decided that he would like to return home. This was not unnatural, as we had already been one year away and had not even yet arrived at the point which we calculated would be the real beginning of our expedition. We must still go several hundred miles east before we could get into the northerly current which we hoped would drift us across the Pole.

I had, therefore, no hesitation in granting him leave to go, nor in repeating the leave when another declared himself willing to accompany him. Indeed, I was rather glad, for one reason, which was that it would give us all an opportunity to send mail home. The journey these two men proposed for themselves was, in their eyes and ours, mere child's play for experienced Northmen like themselves. This was a journey of 500 miles across the snow to Dickson Island – very much less of an undertaking, for example, than my trip from Herschel Island to Fort Egbert, described in an earlier chapter. These boys had the further advantage that they were fully outfitted with everything. As we sailed away, therefore, they waved farewell to us in the best of spirits, and we returned their salute with never a thought but that we should find them waiting for us in Oslo upon our return later. The fates, however, willed it otherwise. One was found dead close to Dickson Island. The other was never heard of. Poor fellows! They were a brave and loyal pair, and their loss will always be sincerely mourned.

Headed eastward, we passed through the strait which lies between the New Siberian Islands and the mainland, and entered the sea to the east of them. The next day, September 20th, we ran against pack ice again, and finding further progress hopeless, we tied up to the ice and spent some time making observations to determine the direction and the rate of the drift. These measurements showed a very strong current southward. This, of course, meant that we should soon be driven again on the mainland. We resolved to seek the first opportunity to move forward and seek shelter around Cape Shelasky. Luck was against us, and we succeeded only in getting as far as Aijon Island where we were caught fast on September 23d. Here we drove head-on fifty yards into the ice and again made ready for a winter's stay.

Natives were soon descried on the Island, and from these Tsjuktsji, as these Siberian aborigines are called, we bought a large number of caribou for our winter's supply of fresh meat. These people apparently are of much the same blood as the Eskimos of the North American and Greenland coasts, but their language is utterly different. There is no communication between these two branches except in the neighbourhood of Bering Strait. There, a few Eskimos from Alaska have crossed the Strait and settled on the north coast of Siberia. They have carried on sufficient intercourse with their Asiatic brothers so that many representatives of each tribe speak the other's language; and there has been, I believe, some intermarriage.

Dr Sverdrup, the scientist of our expedition, decided to seize the opportunity of our winter's stay to go southward into Siberia to gather scientific material about the *Tsjuktsji* and their country. He therefore joined up with a native tribe and travelled southward with them, returning to the *Maud* in the middle of the following May. Dr Sverdrup has written a fascinating book describing the very important scientific observations which he made on this expedition.

When the ice broke up in July I decided to push on to Nome. There were several good reasons for this decision. First, we should be glad to take on supplies and make repairs. Second, our experience thus far had indicated that we should have to go on anyhow practically to Bering Strait before we should be able to enter the ice. And finally, my heart action was still unsatisfactory after more than a year's opportunity to recuperate from my experience in the observatory with the kerosene lamp, and I was glad of an opportunity to consult a specialist. We made the journey from Aijon to Nome without incident and arrived in August.

At Nome four more of the boys decided to leave the expedition. This left the *Maud* with only myself as commander, Dr Sverdrup the scientist, Wisting and Olonkin. Perhaps we took something of a risk in setting forth again with a ship as large as the *Maud* and only four men to handle her in an emergency. But we were all experienced, none of us had any fears of the outcome, and nothing untoward which mere numbers could have prevented happened to mar our journey. The misfortune that did befall us was the breaking of the propeller after we had rounded Cape Serdze Kamen (Dog's-Head). This accident compelled us to winter on the Cape, where the gathering of the land ice pushed us ashore and the breaking up of the ice later thrust us off again without any damage to the well-designed *Maud*.

During the winter, we had for neighbours three tents of the native Tsjuktsji. Of course, we became well acquainted with them, and not until we had done so did I venture to inquire regarding the most interesting of the three families. This home group consisted of an old man, an old woman, and a boy of six. One day, I inquired of the woman, "Is that your child?" taking it for granted she would say that he was a grandchild whose parents had perished. To my astonishment, her answer was simply, "Yes." She must have read my surprise in my face, for she added, "My husband had him." She then explained the situation fully. She said that, though she and her husband had married young, as is the custom of these people (Eskimos and Tsjuktsji are affianced by their parents in infancy and frequently set up housekeeping as man and wife at the age of thirteen), they had continued childless into middle life and on until it was certain they would never have a family. This was a great disappointment to them both, and one day the wife said to the husband, "We must not grow old without children in the house. So-and-so (naming another member of the tribe) has a very nice wife. Go and tell him about our wish for a child and see if he will not let her bear it for us."

The husband did as the wife bade him, and the accommodating friend agreed to the proposal. The result was the six-year-old lad about whom I had inquired, who, while he was his father's son by blood, was equally his mother's son by the love which had brought about his existence. Informal marital relations are not uncommon among these Northern natives. They are, perhaps, to be ascribed less to an undeveloped moral sense than to the exigencies of life that beset a sparse population struggling against terrific odds for their existence.

As the winter wore on, the men in this settlement became greatly attached to us and we to them. When the spring thaw should come, our first concern would be, of course, to get the *Maud* back to Seattle for repairs. Pondering upon the necessity of working the ship through the ice under sail, I decided that it would be wise to add to our crew. I therefore asked five of the men if they would be willing to accompany us when we made our start. Their reply touched me to the heart. "Anywhere you go, we will go with you; anything you ask us to do, we will do – except, if you asked us to commit suicide, we would ask you to repeat your question." I joyfully took them at their word, and they remained with us for a year as most useful men and loyal helpers.

No task was too heavy or hours too long for them. They were calm and cheerful in every situation. But when we reached Seattle, the noise of the city nearly drove two of them insane, and they could not rest until they were free to return on a northbound steamer which would set them down on the Siberian mainland, whence they could make their way overland to their home. After I had paid them off, the oldest of them asked for some beads. I was astonished.

"What in the world," thought I, "can they want with beads, when their women folk already have all they could possibly need?"

One of the men explained. "On our way back home along Siberia, we shall have cross deep rivers, and one never knows whether the gods of the rivers may be angry and let us down through a weak spot in the ice that we cannot see. Therefore, we should like a few beads to give to the gods of the rivers so that they may let us pass in safety."

To go back a moment to Cape Dog's-Head, before we started on our return to Nome: when I chose the five Tsjuktsji to make the voyage with us, the trader on the place rather objected to one of the men, who was named Kakot. He thought him rather a sorry-looking fellow, who, he said, was "just no good." I did not agree with him, though there was something about Kakot that made him rather a pathetic figure.

Kakot came to me one day and asked for a leave of absence. When I inquired the reason, he explained that he wanted to go several days' journey to the north to visit a related tribe and see his little daughter before he went on the long journey. He had lost his wife, and the child had been taken by a cousin whose wife had agreed to bring her up as her own child. Kakot had got word that this Northern tribe was suffering for lack of food, and he was afraid his child was starving.

I could well believe his story, for game was very scarce on the coast that year, and our visit to the Cape had been a godsend to our own group of native neighbours, with whom we had shared enough of our food to eke out their insufficient store.

I readily consented to Kakot's journey, and he disappeared. When he did not return at the end of the week he had specified as his furlough, I started to wonder. I did not lose faith, however. My confidence was justified three days later when, in the dusk, as I came on the deck of the *Maud*, I found Kakot standing on the deck.

"Where is the child?" I asked him.

He pointed to the deck near the rail where a bundle of fur lay on the boards.

"Bring her here," I told him.

Kakot picked up the bundle and put it in my arms. I carried it into the cabin to the light and called my companions. When we opened the bundle, a pathetic sight was disclosed – a little five-year-old Eskimo baby, stark naked, every bone showing from starvation, her body covered from head to foot with sores. Her hair was matted and was alive with "cooties."

The first thing we did for her was to give her a bath and cut her hair short In passing, I might remind the reader that no Eskimo ever voluntarily takes a bath from birth to death. Kakot's little daughter, therefore, is one of the few Eskimos in history who has bathed. We next washed the sores with a solution of tar and alcohol, made some proper clothes for her, and set about feeding her up. In a few weeks, she looked another person. The sores disappeared, her flesh filled out, and she was a thoroughly charming, bright-eyed little creature. I persuaded Kakot to bring her with him on our voyage to Seattle.

On our way thither, we stopped at East Cape in Bering Strait and visited an Australian trader named Carpendale. He was a keen, blue-eyed Australian who had married a native woman and had had by her several children. Among them was a girl aged nine. I told him that I should like to take her as a companion for Kakot's daughter and send the two of them together to school in Norway. This would give the girls the advantages of travel and education, while, on the other hand, it would be of the greatest interest to scientists to study their characteristics and to observe their mental possibilities. Mr Carpendale agreed, so, when I reached Norway in 1922, I had with me these two children, aged five and nine, and put them in school. There they remained for two years. At the end of that time, when I came to take them back to their own people, their teachers told me that each was the brightest pupil in her class.

In appearance, the two girls formed a striking contrast. Kakot's daughter, with her black hair and eyes, had a perfect white skin. Carpendale's daughter, on the other hand, had a very dark brown colour. Naturally, the girls attracted the greatest attention, not only in Oslo but also on their first arrival in civilization in Seattle and on their journey across the United States and the Atlantic.

CHAPTER VI

Financial Worries

While the *Maud* was undergoing repairs and taking on provisions in Seattle, I returned to Norway to raise further funds. This was in the January of 1922. I was much gratified to learn that in my absence the Norwegian Parliament had granted me 500,000 kroner to finance the continuance of the *Maud* expedition. This was doubly pleasant because it was done without even an intimation from me, much less solicitation, and I was therefore the more deeply grateful. By a sheer chance, however, which the donors could not have foreseen, this sum had become inadequate by the time I arrived to claim it. The post-war deflation, which affected the currencies of so many nations, had caused a radical decline in the value of the krone. By this decline, the grant, when I received it, had fallen in purchasing power to only one half what it had been before, or to the equivalent of about $75,000. I was disappointed but not disheartened, and determined to try to proceed with my work, with the hope that fortune would favour me as in the past, and that I should somehow find means to finance the trip.

I had now become obsessed completely with the vision of a new method of attacking the Arctic problem, a method which, I felt sure, would revolutionize the whole practice of Arctic exploration. The reader will recall that twelve years earlier I had engaged an airplane pilot to assist me in my Polar work. The reader will also recall that, five years later, I had bought a Farman airplane for use in the North, but had made a gift of this airplane to the Norwegian government when the World War broke out in 1914. Now, in 1922, I was more than ever convinced that the time had come to adopt this new method in the North.

Earlier in this book I have explained the revolutionary significance of Nansen's Polar methods – how his use of light sledges and dog teams had indicated to all who followed him the secret of success in long fast dashes to the Poles. For myself I claim a similar innovation in the use of aircraft for Arctic exploration. In a later chapter, I shall enlarge upon this subject, which involves the whole predictable future of Arctic exploration. For present purposes, however, it suffices merely to mention the point.

When I prepared to return to Seattle in 1922 to rejoin the *Maud*, I determined to take with me aircraft for use in the Arctic. I heard while in Oslo of the then new type of Junker 'plane which had just taken the world's record for continuous flight by remaining in the air twenty-seven hours without landing. I saw in this record an opportunity to realize the ambition which had become fixed in my mind, namely, to fly from continent to continent across the Polar Sea. I resolved to make the attempt to fly from Point Barrow, on the north coast of Alaska, to Spitzbergen, to the north of Norway. I had no interest in the Pole itself – Peary's splendid achievement in 1909 had destroyed the value of that prize for all later explorers.

The crossing of the Arctic Ocean, however, was still a virgin opportunity. It was also an undertaking of the greatest scientific importance. The largest of the earth's surfaces (land or water) that yet lay unexplored was that part of the Arctic Ocean which stretches between the north coast of Alaska, past the North Pole, and on to northern Europe. The scientific importance of exploring it is this: The Poles are the "climate makers" of the temperate zones – the air currents that wheel about the ends of the earth have more effect upon the temperature day by day in New York and Paris than any other influence except the sun alone. A knowledge of Polar geography and meteorology is therefore of vast importance to scientists as data for their understanding of the origins of these air currents.

My interest, therefore, in this North transoceanic flight was not in mere adventure. It was geographical and scientific.

I gratified my desire for a Junker 'plane by buying one in New York and taking it to Seattle with me when I returned there in the spring of 1922. I stopped in New York on my way to Seattle, and there I discussed my plans for Polar flight with the officers of the Curtiss Aeroplane Company at Garden City, Long Island. They understood my reasons for buying the Junker 'plane – its tremendous cruising radius and its fireproof construction. The Junker derived both of these qualities largely from the material used in its construction, as it was built wholly of a new metal, duralumin, which combined approximately the lightness of aluminum with the strength of steel. Mr C. M. Keys, president of the Curtiss Company, shared my enthusiasm for studying the Arctic from the air, and he very generously offered me a Curtiss Oriole to be used as an auxiliary 'plane for shorter reconnaissance flights. I gratefully accepted his offer, and later made good use of the Oriole in the North.

After my arrival in Seattle, all the preparations for the expedition were soon finished. We were fully provisioned for seven years. We had also a complete set of new instruments of the latest design for making scientific observations. We left Seattle on June 1, 1922. The ice conditions were just as bad this summer as in all the previous summers, and arriving at Deering, Alaska, I heard that a trading schooner was at

Kotzebue Sound on her way to Point Barrow. I then decided to see the skipper and with him discuss the possibility of transferring the big Junker 'plane to her, so that the *Maud* could proceed to the pack ice and start her drift as soon as possible. This was done, and Lieutenant Omdal and myself, with the Junker 'plane, were transferred to the schooner and proceeded to the northwest along the coast of Alaska, while the *Maud,* under the command of Captain Wisting, went straight north into the drift ice. On account of the bad ice condition, the schooner did not reach Point Barrow, but had to land us at Wainwright Inlet.

I had taken advantage of a short stay in London in the preceding February to visit a distinguished heart specialist to see what permanent injury, if any, had been done me by my experience with the leaky kerosene lamp at Maud Harbour in the winter of 1918-I9. His verdict was brief and emphatic – "No more expeditions!" and he added,"' If you expect to live more than a few years longer you must avoid all strenuous exercise."

Nine months later, however, on November 19, 1922, I started on foot from Point Barrow through the snow with a native mail carrier and made the run of 500 miles to Kotzebue in ten days, or at an average speed of 50 miles a day. The next two days I ran 90 miles from Kotzebue to Deering; and in the four days following that, I ran 200 miles from Deering to Nome. In other words, after having been "counted out" by a heart specialist in February, I did the hardest travelling of my life in November, covering practically 800 miles through the snow at an average speed of nearly 50 miles a day, stopping only a few hours every night to sleep.

That was five years ago, and though I have since then had several severe tests of physical endurance, I have never yet experienced any unpleasant results from my exertions. I tell this, not to belittle an excellent doctor or to boast of myself, but to remark the marvellous recuperative powers of the human body when its owner follows, as I have done, a conscientious regimen of life from youth onward to preserve it in the prime condition in which nature intended it to function.

I spent the winter of 1922–23 in Nome, leaving there in April and arriving back in Wainwright on May 12, 1923. I found that Lieutenant Omdal had improved the long wait by working on the Junker, and that he had it all ready to fly. He had attached the skis, which had been designed to take the place of wheels for landing on the ice. Soon after my arrival, he undertook a trial flight. When he came down, the left ski crumpled like a piece of cardboard. An examination showed that it had been so designed that all the pressure of the impact at one point in the underrigging was concentrated upon a portion of the metal not much thicker than a heavy sheet of paper. We had no facilities for making repairs of this sort, and, anyhow, it was clear that another gear, of a better design, would have to be employed if we were to hope for successful landings. The only alternative was to try a pair of pontoons that we had, which, of course, were intended for landing in the water. They proved at once to be unserviceable. I decided, therefore, to stay at Wainright and to send Omdal back to Seattle for new landing gear.

At this point, I ran full steam into a series of events that led to the most distressing, the most humiliating, and altogether the most tragic episode of my life. Two years earlier, my good friend the Norwegian Consul at Seattle had recommended to me there a citizen of Danish birth named H. H. Hammer. This Dane was a ship broker in Seattle. He was very resourceful and energetic. He had a wide acquaintance in the city, and he bore a good reputation. One of my friends, after the events about to be chronicled had transpired, characterized Hammer as "a criminal optimist." This characterization should preface the narrative that follows, because it accurately reflects my own judgment of Hammer, now that I look back, and because it will help the reader preserve a true perspective upon what happened.

When I was first introduced to Hammer in 1921, I had no reason to suspect him of anything but sincere friendliness to me and to the cause of Arctic exploration. He was extremely useful to us during that winter, in helping to buy the provisions and make the repairs to the *Maud*'s propeller when we were getting ready for the start to the Polar region.

Now, to resume my narrative: When I had about decided to send Omdal back for new landing gear and myself to remain, I got a telegram from Hammer which said in effect: "Come on out. I have three new 'planes at your disposal." I was naturally overjoyed at this unexpected news, and hastened to obey the summons. I made all haste to Seattle, where I met Hammer and talked over the situation with him.

To my sorrow, I was now about to learn that another qualification of an explorer – and unfortunately one which, in the nature of things, it is impossible for him to acquire – is a familiarity with business. The disaster into which I was rapidly being plunged was due wholly to my lack of business experience. I had never had any opportunity to acquaint myself with business methods and had always had to rely upon others for the management of any business details. Thus far, my trust in others in these matters had never caused me any trouble. I did what I was told, and everything came out all right. But not so in my connection with Hammer.

Our conversation developed that Hammer had gone to Berlin for medical treatment and to undergo an operation. At least, that was the reason he gave out when he went. What he actually did was to go to the Junker factory in Germany, and, with his ready tongue, talk the Junker people into giving outright a new 'plane of later design and better construction.

I appreciated the generosity of the Junker people, but I had now become convinced, from our experience at Point Barrow, that the Junker 'plane could not make the flight, and that the only hope of success lay in getting flying boats. In other words, I had concluded that efforts to land on the very rough Arctic ice with skis or similar devices was not practical. We must have airplanes specially designed to light on and take off from the water, snow, and ice.

Hammer now offered to get the flying boats. The next question was, where to get the money? Hammer assured me that he would get it, and he now unfolded a most ingenious plan.

He would sell to the public postcards of the thinnest possible paper, to be carried over the Pole on the trans-Polar Sea flight, so that the purchaser could surprise and please a friend by having him receive a card carried for the first time over the Pole by air. These cards were later made up and were sold for one dollar apiece. Hammer ultimately disposed of about ten thousand of them.

Meanwhile, I proceeded on to Europe, and at Hammer's insistence I gave him – how unwisely I was later to learn – a power of attorney to transact business in my name. I went first to Oslo, and with great difficulty persuaded the Norwegian government to issue a special stamp to be used on these postcards. The government allowed me to buy the whole issue of these stamps and to resell them for what I could get, using the difference to finance the flight. The stamps would be the source of considerable income, for philatelists had hitherto classified Norway as almost unique in the purity of its series of postage stamps, since Norway had hitherto practically never used a novelty stamp of any kind. For this reason, the Polar stamp would have an especial interest and value to collectors.

While I was in Oslo, engaged in this work, Hammer arrived in Europe, and we went to Copenhagen, where we had a meeting with the people of the Dornier aeroplane factory. The flying boat built by this firm was the 'plane I had decided was the most suitable for the flight. Hammer promptly ordered, not one, but three of these boats, and contracted to pay $40,000 apiece for them. With his glib tongue, he persuaded the Dornier people, as he had persuaded me, that the funds were available; and they actually proceeded to design and build the three 'planes on his order without more than a nominal deposit on account. Hammer in reality had only about $10,000, but with his "criminal optimism" it is entirely possible that he felt certain of getting the rest in time to make the payments. Hammer reassured me with convincing eloquence that the money would be forthcoming. I therefore devoted myself hopefully to raising as much money on my part as I could from the sale of stamps.

The Dornier people built the 'planes in a factory at Marina de Pisa in Italy, as at that time the Germans, by the terms of the Peace Treaty, were not permitted to build aeroplanes of that size in Germany.

I did not begin to suspect Hammer in the slightest degree until I went to Marina de Pisa in the spring of 1924 to inspect the 'planes and to witness their trial flights. There I began to hear disturbing quotations of things Hammer had been saying to the Italians. Apparently, he had been doing a good deal of bragging and had been giving out other irresponsible talk. My suspicions were aroused, but there was nothing tangible enough to cause me to take sharp issue with him.

A little later, however, some of my own Norwegian boys, in whose word I had every confidence, from years of experience with them, told me some specific stories of things Hammer was saying. For example, he was boasting that he had made twenty-one flights at Spitzbergen, and furthermore that he was going to fly one of the 'planes to the Pole. Nothing could be more preposterous than either of these statements. He was as ignorant as a greengrocer of anything about the operation of an airplane; and he was even more ignorant, if that were possible, of anything about navigation. Nothing could have been more absurd than the idea of taking such an utterly inexperienced person as he upon an expedition which at best was fraught with the greatest hazards, and which would call at the minimum for previous experience in the Arctic, which he had never had.

These and other stories became so numerous and explicit that I was finally compelled to wire him and order the whole expedition cancelled. I was furiously angry, and I emphatically "fired" him from all connection with the expedition and with my business concerns. I published to the world the fact that I had broken all connection with Hammer. He immediately realized that other things which he had done, and it which he had involved my name, would now come to light and would be extremely unpleasant. Evidently his conscience did not justify his actions, for he did not stay to meet them. Instead of flying over the North Pole, he "flew" to Japan.

As soon as I discovered Hammer's unreliability and had disowned him publicly, naturally, everybody with whom he had done business informed me of the commitments he had made in my name. What this information showed was enough to have taxed the resources even of a man experienced in business. To me, to whom business has always been a mystery, this situation was nothing short of appalling. I was humiliated beyond my power to express it, because Hammer, by making commitments far beyond any resources I could possibly muster, had placed me in a position in the eyes of the world of being a financial scoundrel.

My cup of bitterness, however, was yet to be filled further to overflowing. My brother Leon had managed my personal business from the time I first undertook my career of exploration. I sent to him all money I made and all the bills I ran up. He attended to the banking and the payment of debts. He kept the book of accounts of all my business, which I never inspected, as I had the fullest confidence in him. This brother, in my misfortune, turned against me. I say it with shame – I would not discuss it publicly were it not that his betrayal led to action in the courts which made it common knowledge in Norway.

It appeared from my brother's books that I owed him about $25,000. I have no doubt that, under ordinary circumstances, he would have confidently permitted this debt to stand until my lectures and writings enabled me to repay it. But the sudden appearance on the scene of the other debts that Hammer had placed against my name here, there, and everywhere frightened my brother into the belief that my debt to him would be lost in the catastrophe. Instead of doing what he could to help me fund these debts, so that I could have time to work them out, he tried a desperate stratagem to collect his money ahead of the other creditors. My only asset was my home near Oslo, and my brother declared that he would take measures to sell my house for the satisfaction of my debt to him.

I was grieved to the heart at his turning against me, but was also furious at his rapacity. I immediately sought legal advice. My lawyer assured me that my brother's plan to sell my house would be treated by the courts as a criminal attempt to defraud the other creditors. He therefore relieved my mind on that score. I now demanded access to the books, but he angrily refused. With my other creditors pressing me and making it necessary that I know exactly the extent of my debts in order to work out a plan of meeting them, it was essential that I should have access to my brother's books.

There were two things to do – either obtain a court order for an examination of the books or go into bankruptcy. I preferred the latter alternative. The Court would then subpoena the books for its own information, and my brother would have to bring them out. I viewed the prospect of public bankruptcy proceedings with inexpressible shame, but, as there seemed to be no alternative, I decided to do so.

My brother's books were then produced by order of the Court; all my other debts were made of court record.[1]

I was now penniless, and it was only by a mercy of the law that I had a shelter over my head. This, however, was the least of my sorrows. The little Norwegian nation, to which I had more than once brought a new fame by reason of my explorations, had time and again been delighted to do me honour. Now that ignorance had led me into a humiliating position, the Norwegians, almost to a man, turned upon me with unbelievable ferocity. Men who had praised and flattered me now stooped to circulating the basest scandal. The Norwegian press attacked me. They could not take from me the glory of the Northwest Passage, nor the discovery of the South Pole – achievements to call which less than illustrious would convict even myself of false modesty if I described them otherwise. But now that I was helpless and embarrassed, the same lips that had described my career as a glory of the nation did not scruple to repeat lies of the most transparent fabrication, in a cruel effort to besmirch my private character and tarnish my name. Some even declared that my bankruptcy was a conspiracy with my brother to defraud my creditors! More vicious minds concocted the story that the two Eskimo girls that I had brought to Norway were my illegitimate children, whose paternity I had falsely ascribed to Kakot and the Australian trader – an invention so transparent that, if my misfortunes had not made normally sensible people credulous of any fantastic tale, it would have been merely amusing, in the light of my known whereabouts in regions remote from their birthplaces for years both before and after the possible date of their origins.

The tragedy of my situation at that time, three short years ago, words cannot express. After thirty years of labour and achievement, after a life devoted to a rigorous code of honour, to have a misplaced confidence in a man of business cause my name to be dragged in the mire of the basest scandal and suspicion, was an intolerable humiliation. Undoubtedly, I was guilty of a grave mistake in trusting my business concerns so implicitly to others, though I do not see how I could have done otherwise than trust them to somebody. For that mistake I deserved the punishment of bankruptcy, but certainly I did not deserve the contumely and ingratitude of my countrymen. Toward those who seized upon my misfortune as an opportunity to destroy with slander a fellow man – whose chief crime in their eyes was that he had achieved an eminence greater than theirs – for those who took pleasure in their slander because they hoped thereby to tear down one who had risen high, I feel an infinite contempt and an inexpressible scorn: I thank Heaven it has given me the opportunity, since those days, to achieve results in exploration that have demonstrated anew my character and my serious purpose in life. Also, that I have been permitted to retain the esteem of those men of real understanding of my character and purposes, who have been above being influenced by traducers, and who have generously made possible my last achievements. Neither can I ever be grateful enough to my Sovereign, His Majesty King Haakon VII, whose unflinching confidence in me has solaced my every hour.

In the fall of 1924, I came to the United States to recoup my fortunes by lecturing and writing for the newspapers. In my syndicated articles, which were published by newspapers in many parts of the United States, I suggested that dirigible balloons were the coming means of traversing the Arctic regions for scientific exploration. Reconnaissance flights in heavier-than-air machines were possible, and would be useful in learning the general geographical nature of the problems. But protracted study of these problems would call for the use of dirigibles, because of their greater safety. Heavier-than-air machines, I pointed out, would not be useful for this purpose until the helicopter should be perfected, making it possible for airplanes to hover and to land slowly by vertical descent.

My private hopes for my next expedition were necessarily limited to a reconnaissance flight from continent to continent across the North Pole, for the very simple reason that airplanes were cheaper than dirigibles. In the embarrassed state of my finances, and under the cloud of misrepresentation that had settled on my name, I should be hard put to it even to acquire the lesser backing needed to organize an aeroplane flight.

My depression reached its climax upon my return to New York from a lecture tour. The tour was practically a financial failure. My newspaper articles had produced but little revenue. As I sat in my room in the Waldorf-Astoria, it seemed to me as if the future had closed solidly against me, and that my career as an explorer had come to an inglorious end. Courage, will power, indomitable faith – these qualities had carried me through many dangers and to many achievements. Now even their merits seemed of no avail. I was nearer to black despair than ever before in my fifty-four years of life.

As I sat in my room, musing in this way, the telephone rang. I answered it, and a strange man's voice inquired if he might not come up and see me, adding, "I met you several years ago in France, during the war." Hundreds of idle people have greeted me with this kind of an introduction, their only purpose being to waste my time in useless conversation. There was now even more reason for my gruff and non-committal response, for I had been having painful experience with callers who came to serve summonses, and with others who had come to discuss Hammer's debts. I was in no mood to receive casual acquaintances whose only credentials were ready references to "an introduction in France."

My caller's next sentence, however, gave me a pleasant start. He said: "I am an amateur interested in exploration, and I might be able to supply some money for another expedition." Needless to say, I bade him come up at once. Five minutes later, I was deep in conversation with Mr Lincoln Ellsworth, whose name needs no introduction to the world.

CHAPTER VII

An Airplane Flight
With Lincoln Ellsworth

Mr Ellsworth explained that he had an independent income and a strong thirst for adventure. If I would consent to share the command of an expedition with him, so that he might enjoy the fun of flying across the Arctic Ocean, he would undertake to provide the funds for the purchase of the two flying boats and for some of the other expenses.

I was delighted. The gloom of the past year rolled away, and even the horrors of my business experience faded into forgetfulness in the activities of preparation.

Mr Ellsworth supplied $85,000 in cash.

I arranged for a pilot and a mechanician for each 'plane. The flying boats were delivered at Kings Bay, Spitzbergen, in the spring of 1925. By May 4th, everything was practically ready for the flight, and on that date we all gathered in Spitzbergen. There were Ellsworth and myself; Riiser-Larsen and Dietrichson, the pilots; and Omdal and Feucht, the mechanicians. When we gathered for our first council of war, Riiser-Larsen gave us a piece of information that was quite startling. He said that he had discovered that the Italian dirigible N-I could be purchased from the Italian government, and that the price would be certainly not more than $100,000. We were all delighted as well as astonished. It had never occurred to Ellsworth or myself that a dirigible could be got at anything like so reasonable a price. We should never have been content with the flying boats if we had known this fact. Our objective was a complete crossing of the Arctic Ocean from continent to continent by way of the North Pole. With the flying boats, this was a hazardous possibility, and we were glad to risk the hazards for the sake of the possibility. But, with a dirigible, success was a reasonable certainty.

Ellsworth on the spot promised $100,000 for the purchase of the *N-1* if Riiser-Larsen could confirm his news of the opportunity to buy it. We decided to continue our present flight in the flying boats, but agreed in any event to make the flight by dirigible the following summer.

I had an especial reason for being delighted about the news of the *N-1* for I had been aboard her two years before as a guest and had made a short flight. I had followed her later career and was aware that she had made many successful flights, demonstrating that her cruising radius was quite sufficient to assure the journey across the Arctic Ocean. Minor changes in design would have to be made. Particularly, a stiff nose would have to be substituted for the present soft nose, in order to make it possible to moor her to a mast instead of harbouring her in a covered hangar. I was exultant at the thought that now at last my long dream of an Arctic transoceanic flight was in sight of coming true.

We named our two Dornier flying boats the *N-24* and the *N-25*. Ellsworth, Dietrichson, and Omdal were assigned to the *N-24* as navigator, pilot, and mechanician respectively, while myself, Riiser-Larsen, and Feucht discharged the corresponding duties on the *N-25*.

We left Spitzbergen May 21, 1925, and shaped our course to carry us toward the North Pole. Now that we were sure of accomplishing our continent-to-continent purpose the following year in a dirigible, we planned to make the present venture only an extended reconnaissance flight. We would study carefully the nature of the ice surface as far toward the Pole as we could reach, especially with an eye to possible landing places. Of course, also, this particular part of the Arctic Ocean was yet unexplored, and we might possibly make some discovery about land besides.

Each flying boat carried fuel for a flight of 600 miles and return. When we had reached 88 degrees north latitude – or approximately 600 miles from Spitzbergen – we saw below us the first bit of open water that we had observed in the whole distance travelled. To make sure that even this was not an optical illusion, we circled low about it. As we did so, the N-25 developed engine trouble and was forced to make a landing. If ever a landing place appeared providentially for a 'plane, this was the occasion. At any other moment in our previous flight of 600 miles, our landing would have had to be made upon the roughest kind of hummocks with the almost certain destruction of our 'planes.

As it was, the bit of water to which we descended was barely long enough to permit our landing without accident. Our boats stopped against the ice at the end of the pool, but fortunately had lost so much momentum that no damage was caused.

We set feverishly to work trying to save the N-25. We soon discovered a desperate incentive for haste the water upon which we had alighted was freezing over. Within six hours of our landing, it was closed up solid. By strenuous work, we had kept the boat free from the clutches of the ice.

We were now in a thoroughly dangerous situation. Here we were, 600 miles from civilization, landed upon the ice with airplanes equipped for landing upon water, with the engine of one of the 'planes utterly out of commission, and with provisions adequate for full nourishment for only about three weeks.

The only prospect of salvation lay in transferring the whole party to the N-24 and making every effort to get that one 'plane into the air again. Under the best possible conditions for rising, this would have been no easy matter, with twice the number of men the N-24 was supposed to carry. But we did not have the best possible conditions. Instead of rising from the water, as our boats were designed to do, we must rise from the surface of the ice. And that surface was not smooth like a skating pond, but was as rough as hummocks could make it-hummocks of every size that were heaped together in utter confusion.

There was nothing for us to do but to try to flatten out enough of this ice surface to make a runway long enough to permit us to get up sufficient momentum to rise. We worked furiously for twenty-four days at this task. It was truly a race with death, for ultimate starvation could not much longer have been delayed. As it was, we lived on eight ounces of food a day, which is just one half the ration that Peary fed to each of his dogs on his dash to the Pole. Every morning we had a small cake of chocolate dissolved in hot water, making one cup of very weak cocoa, and three crackers, each about the size of a Nabisco wafer. For dinner we had a cup of soup. For supper we had another cup of "near cocoa" and three more biscuits. Of course, we suffered somewhat from unsatisfied appetite, but, on the other hand, it was amazing to see how we maintained our strength on such a meagre diet while performing such strenuous labour.

On the twenty-fourth day we had succeeded in getting a runway more or less level and 500 metres long. The N-25 theoretically required 1,500 metres of open water in which to get up momentum enough to rise. We could not, however, level off more than 500 metres. At the end of that distance our runway dropped off with an abrupt edge to the surface of a very small pool of water about three feet below and about fifteen feet broad. On the other side was a flat cake of ice about 150 feet in diameter and on the far side of which rose a hummock at least twenty feet high. This, of course, was beyond our strength to break down. As it was, I should estimate that we moved at least 500 tons of ice in the twenty-four days.

Such rest as we took from the heavy work of digging snow was spent partly in sleep (though we got precious little of that) but chiefly in making astronomical observations and depth soundings. These soundings conclusively, demonstrated that there was no land near the region where we were. They

106

were made by the use of a new and most ingenious German device which weighed only three pounds. This device utilized the echo principle. Two holes were bored through the ice. Through one of them was dropped a length of wire attached to a very sensitive telephone receiving microphone.

One man listened in on this device while, at the other hole, another man fired a submerged charge of explosive. Synchronized stop watches were used to take the exact time of the explosion and of the "echo." The vibration set up by the explosion was transmitted by the water to the bed of the ocean, whence, by rebound, it returned through the water to the surface where it, was perceptible in the ear pieces attached to the submerged wire.

We took two soundings with this device, and in each case five seconds elapsed between the sound of the explosion and the sound of its echo from the ocean bed. This five-seconds interval indicated that the ocean at this point is about 12,000 feet deep. Naturally, no land exists very close to water of such depth.

By June 15th, everything that could be done to get the *N-25* ready had been done. We had transferred from the *N-24* everything useful for the return flight that we could safely attempt to carry in the already overburdened *N-25*. All six of us men stowed ourselves in the crowded cockpit with the motor running and Riiser-Larsen at the "stick." At the signal to go, Riiser-Larsen opened the throttle to the limit and we began moving along our uneven runway of ice.

The most anxious moments of my life were the next few seconds. As we gained speed, the inequalities on the ice multiplied their effect upon us and the fuselage swayed from side to side with such a careening motion that more than once I feared we should be thrown over on one side and have one of our wings crushed. Nearer and faster we approached the end of our runway, but still the bumping motion indicated we had not left the ice. Still gaining momentum but still hugging the ice, we approached the brink of the little drop off into the pool. We reached the pool, jumped over it, dashed down on the flat cake, and then we rose. An enormous sense of relief swept over me, but it lasted only an instant. There, dead ahead of us, and only a few yards away, loomed the twenty-foot hummock on the far side of the little pool. We were headed straight toward it. Five seconds would tell whether we should clear it and at least be in the free air with a fighting chance to return to safe haven, or whether we should crash into it. Should we crash – even if we escaped instant death – we should be faced with the certainty of ultimate death marooned on the Arctic ice. Thoughts and sensations crowd fast at such a moment. The seconds seemed terrible hours. But we did clear it – we could not have had more than an inch to spare. At last we were on the way, after twenty-four days of desperate work and anxiety.

Hour after hour we flew southward. Were we on the right course? Would our fuel last if we were? Lower and lower the fuel gage sank. At length, with only a half-hour's supply of gasoline left, a mighty shout went up from all of us. There, far below us, to the south, lay the familiar peaks of Spitzbergen. Below us appeared a streak of black which meant open water for a landing. Our troubles were not yet over. To reach this water we must make a wide sweep over hummocky ice. This would require some manoeuvring of the 'plane. I had been watching Riiser-Larsen, our pilot, for the last half-hour, and had noticed that when he worked the aileron control it appeared that he had to use unwonted force on the lever. Finally, he had shouted to me that this control was out of order. We had now to come right down, but fortunately we had first reached the open water. If not, we would all have been crushed right there and then.

It was almost as close a call as our experience of the weeks before.

That was the end of our first long flight over the Arctic Ocean to 88° north latitude.

CHAPTER VIII

The Transpolar Flight
Of The *Norge*

The inside story of the *Norge's* flight over the North Pole in the summer of 1926 has never been told. I would not tell it now were it not that so much misrepresentation has been broadcast about it that simple justice to myself and my companions compels me to reveal all the facts.

There is, of course, an inside story to every undertaking. Wherever a group of men get together to do a difficult task, misunderstandings are bound to arise, clashes of temperament occur, incidents happen that are best forgotten. Polar expeditions are no exception to this rule. I have yet to hear of one that did not have such episodes – not only my own expeditions, but all others with which I am familiar. It is a pleasant and proper trait of human nature to try to forget these things when success has crowned one's efforts, and to bury them in the agreeable oblivion of mutual felicitation.

Such has been my instinct. Always, heretofore, after every expedition, I have written a book describing it, but never before have I included in a book any of these unpleasant incidental matters.

However, I must for once break this rule. It is no only that the provocation this time is greater. I could let that pass. But if I should leave the truth about the *Norge's* flight to be gathered by the public from the mass of misrepresentation of the facts which has been poured forth by Italian propaganda, I should be permitting a gross injustice to be visited, not only upon my own reputation, but upon the hard-earned laurels of Mr Lincoln Ellsworth and my Norwegian compatriots who so essentially contributed to the success of that expedition.

I have, therefore, determined in this book to tell the whole story of the *Norge's* flight from its first inception to the finish, unpleasant details and all. By no other means than such an extended and explicit narrative can I produce for permanent record a statement which will give the public a solid basis for understanding the truth about the conflicting stories it has heard.

First of all, let me briefly review the substance of the story. The reader of the preceding chapters of this book will realize that a flight from northern Europe to northern Alaska, straight across the Arctic Ocean, and incidentally across the North Pole, had been a dream of mine since 1909, when word reached the world that Admiral Peary had captured the Pole and had left for later explorers only the study of the uncharted Arctic seas. The reader will recall also my numerous attempts to make this passage by air, including my preparations in 1909, 1914, 1922, 1923, 1924, and 1925. He will recall that, in 1925, at Spitzbergen, Riiser-Larsen had brought word to Ellsworth and me that the Italian dirigible *N-I* could possibly be purchased at a price that we could afford to pay, and that Ellsworth had then offered to contribute $100,000 if we could buy her.

In the light of these years of planning for the flight across the Arctic, how preposterous is the claim now brazenly sought to be established by the Italians, that Colonel Nobile conceived and engineered the *Norge* expedition, or that he had any other useful function in it than that of pilot of the dirigible!

Nevertheless, precisely this preposterous claim is now assiduously being insinuated into the public consciousness by every art of subtle propaganda. Just how false this fantastic tale really is, I intend to demonstrate in the narrative that follows. I shall give the facts in their chronological order.

The flying boat *N-25* returned to Spitzbergen after the adventure described in the preceding chapter, on the 15th day of June, 1925, and three weeks later, on July 4th, with my five companions, I arrived in Oslo. The expedition we had just concluded having ended without attaining our consistent objective of a continent-to-continent flight, we immediately proceeded with plans for a more ambitious undertaking for the following year. In other words, we set about at once to follow up Riiser-Larsen's intimation that the Italian dirigible *N-I* could be purchased.

We telegraphed to Colonel Nobile, asking him to come to Oslo for a conference. Colonel Nobile, I should explain, was an officer in the Italian Military Air Service, and he was both a designer and a pilot. He had designed the plans from which the dirigible *N-1* was built.

When, therefore, we considered the idea of buying the *N-1* from the Italian government, the obvious thing to do was to consult with Nobile, because he was the man who could answer exactly every question we would raise regarding her cruising radius, lifting power, and all other necessary details for our information. Equally obvious also it would be that, if we bought the *N-1* Nobile would be the ideal man to employ as captain or pilot. He had handled her on many flights, and of course would be familiar with every trick and peculiarity about her.

Colonel Nobile came to Oslo in response to our telegram.

Our first conference was at my home. Riiser-Larsen was also present. Nobile immediately demonstrated that he had come armed with full powers from the Italian government, for he at once made us an offer which astonished us and

111

which in the light of later events was most significant. This offer was that the Italian government would make us a free gift of the *N-1* upon one condition, namely, that we should agree that it should fly the Italian flag.

This offer we instantly rejected. I had not the slightest intention of permitting my dream of seventeen years to be fulfilled under any other flag than that of my native land. I had spent a lifetime learning the art of Polar exploration. I had carried the Norwegian flag through the Northwest Passage and to the South Pole. Nothing could induce me to make the first Arctic Ocean crossing under any other.

It is worth while here to interrupt the narrative for one brief paragraph, to fix in the reader's mind the significance of this offer from the Italian government, delivered to me by an *officer* of its army. I did not realize that significance at the time, but it is now clear that it was a deliberate effort on the part of the government to gain for the present Italian political regime in particular, and for the Italian people in general, a world-wide advertisement. My idea of a transpolar flight was thus subtly to be appropriated as their own by the Italians, and my skill in Arctic exploration was to be utilized as the means of a dramatic achievement for which the Italians would take the credit. Fortunately, my instinct and my pride of race saved me from falling into the trap, even though I did not realize at the time that it was being laid for me. Unfortunately, however, I could not foresee how far the Italians would later stoop in their effort to claim a major share in the honours of the flight. These things came later, and they will appear later in my narrative.

When I had rejected Nobile's offer of the *N-1* as a gift, I asked him the price at which we could purchase it outright, free of all conditions. In reply, he pointed out that the *N-1* had cost the Italian government £20,000 to build. She was now, however, two years old, and though still in good condition had borne the strains of many flights. As her military usefulness was now approaching an end, he was authorized to offer the ship to us for £15,000 and to agree to deliver her to us in perfect condition.

Naturally, we were delighted at this offer. Ellsworth had guaranteed $100,000, and here was the opportunity before me to acquire, for approximately $25,000 less than that, just such an airship as I had dreamed for years of possessing. After a discussion of details, we accepted Nobile's offer.

One of these details was extremely important. The *N-1* was a semi-dirigible, which means that while her gas container was cigar-shaped it was not rigid. This fact involved one serious difficulty. In the absence of a suitable hangar at our prospective landing places, we should need to be able to moor the *N-1* to a mooring mast. With her soft-nosed gas bag, this would be impossible.

We discussed this difficulty, and Nobile agreed that his undertaking to deliver the *N-1* "in perfect condition" should include the alteration of providing her with a stiff nose by which she could be moored to a mast.

Everything having been agreed upon to our mutual satisfaction, Nobile returned to Rome to draw up the final contract. Riiser-Larsen and I were to follow shortly after and sign it.

We two went to Rome the following month (August) and there signed the contract of purchase.

On this visit to Rome there was further discussion of details. I had asked Nobile, in the conference at Oslo the month before, if he would go with us as pilot, and he had agreed. Now, in Rome, he asked that the crew be made up entirely of Italians. To this suggestion I declined positively to agree. I had several reasons. First of all, I intended that the expedition should be primarily a Norwegian-American enterprise, as I had planned it a year before. Ellsworth's financial assistance had made the flight of 1925 possible and would make the flight of 1926 possible. Ellsworth and I had been congenial companions in danger and in achievement. I was delighted to share the national honours with my beloved American friend. I did not intend, however, to share them with the Italians. We owed them nothing but the opportunity to buy and pay for a second-hand military dirigible. I was very glad to be able to hire the Italian officer who had constructed and piloted this ship. But the expedition was Ellsworth's and mine. It was our idea. It was financed with our money, and it would be made in a craft which we had bought and paid for.

Another consideration was this: Riiser-Larsen, the pilot of the *N-25,* and Omdal, the mechanician, had shared our perils in the flying boats, and I intended that they should share the honours in the coming flight. Not only the honours, but also the highly important duties. Riiser-Larsen I considered one of the greatest aviators in the world. His skill and judgment would be invaluable. Omdal was one of the greatest geniuses in practical mechanics, and he, too, would be invaluable in emergencies.

I was determined also to share the flight over the North Pole with Oscar Wisting, one of the gallant four who had accompanied me to the South Pole. I wanted him to share with me the distinction of the incidental crossing of the North Pole on our impending transoceanic flight.

All these considerations were fully explained to Nobile and understood by him. Nobile then asked permission to take five Italian mechanics with us on the flight. He pointed out that the men he had in mind were members of the present crew of the *N-1* and were experienced in handling the motors and operating the gas valves and ballast. In discharging his functions as pilot on the flight, it would greatly simplify Nobile's work if he had under him these men accustomed to handling the craft and able to take their orders in Nobile's native tongue. These points were perfectly reasonable, and I readily assented to his request. It was, therefore, definitely agreed that our expedition should include Nobile and the five Italian mechanics, but no more Italians than these.

An incident of our stay in Rome, on this occasion, gave me my first twinges of apprehension about Nobile. Riiser-Larsen and I wanted to take a trip to the bathing place called Ostia, not far from Rome. Nobile proposed that we make the journey hither as his guests in his automobile. We gratefully accepted the offer.,

This was the wildest ride I have ever taken in any craft. Nobile drove his car. I sat beside him, and Riiser-Larsen's huge frame pretty well filled the rear seat. Nobile proved to be a most eccentric chauffeur. So long as we were proceeding on a straight and level stretch of highway he drove steadily at a rational speed. The moment, however, we approached a curve in the road where an ordinary driver would slow down as a matter of course, Nobile's procedure was directly the opposite. He would press the accelerator down to the floor, and we would take the blind curve at terrific speed. Halfway round, as I was convulsively tightening my grip on the seat with my hands and shuddering with fear of disaster, Nobile would seem to come out of a cloud of abstraction, realize the danger, and frantically seek to avert it. He would jam his brakes on with all his strength, which, of course, with our centrifugal momentum, threatened to topple us over. To prevent this, he would then start zigzagging with the front wheels.

After half a dozen of these exhibitions, I turned to Riiser-Larsen and, speaking in Norwegian, told him the man must be crazy and asked him if he could not make him stop it and tell him how to drive sensibly around curves. Riiser-Larsen, who is one of the bravest as well as one of the most sensible men I ever knew, was sitting muttering to himself that we should certainly all be killed. I realized that, bad as the matter seemed to me, it must seem worse to Riiser-Larsen, who, with his special skill in piloting dangerous vehicles, not only felt the hazards more sensitively than I, but, being used to being at the wheel, felt also more helpless.

After repeated expostulations, we finally persuaded Nobile to observe some semblance of sensible driving, but his whole performance on the round trip was evidence of his extreme nervousness, erratic nature, and lack of balanced judgment. When Riiser-Larsen and I got back to our hotel and were alone, I expressed the gravest apprehensions regarding our wisdom in agreeing to take Nobile as our pilot on the dirigible. If, I exclaimed, this is a sample of his disposition on firm ground, it would be madness for us to trust ourselves with him in the air. Riiser-Larsen's reply astonished me. "No," he said, "that does not follow. Some of the steadiest, coolest aviators I know are men who on the ground have exactly this fellow's nervous characteristics. In ordinary life, they strike you as excitable and erratic. But the moment they take to the air – it may be the steadying effect of the stimulation of danger – their nervousness disappears and they are as cool in an emergency as anyone you could imagine."

Riiser-Larsen's explanation seemed plausible, and I accepted his reassurances – all the more readily because I had observed his own trepidation in the automobile with Nobile. Surely, I thought, if he can believe in this man's capacity in the air after this experience with him on the ground, I need not have doubts about it. Nevertheless, as will appear later in this narrative, Nobile on several occasions during the actual flight across the Arctic revealed exactly the same qualities he had exhibited at the wheel of the motor car, and more than once put us in peril of disaster.

Everything was now arranged. There was nothing more I could do in Italy. The Italians were spending the fall and winter reconditioning the *N-1* and altering the gas bag to provide a stiff nose for mooring. Both Ellsworth and I had many things to occupy us during these next few months.

Ellsworth's father died when we were out on our first flight, and thus he was confronted with the duty of returning to America and transacting the business incidental to closing up his father's estate. I, on my part, must return to the task of raising further money. Ellsworth's contribution insured the purchase of the dirigible and a surplus besides, but I could not stand by and do nothing toward contributing to the other expenses. Furthermore, there were the debts that had caused my bankruptcy. I was then and am still working to pay them, as a matter of honour. I returned, therefore, to America to deliver a series of lectures. My subject was our experiences with the *N-24* and *N-25*. I opened my lecture tour in October and spent the winter travelling across the United States.

When Ellsworth and I realized that we should both have to be away from Europe all that winter, we realized also that questions would arise involving all kinds of detailed negotiations with the Italians over unexpected problems. Equipment for the flight would have to be ordered and assembled. This would involve financial matters. Some competent authority on the ground must be ready to represent our interests, handle our finances, and make decisions.

In this dilemma, we made an arrangement with the Aëro Club of Norway to act for us. At the time, this seemed a fortunate solution. To-day, it is clear enough that it was a mistake of the first magnitude. That, however, was something we could not foresee.

The Aëro Club of Norway was a small organization, unknown outside of Norway. In a small and poor country like Norway, aviation was naturally not a major interest of the population. The military arms of the government had a few 'planes. The Aëro Club, therefore, represented a small amount of tangible aviation interest and an enormous amount of enthusiasm and hope.

The president of the Aëro Club was Dr Rolf Thommessen. He was the editor and owner of one of the largest daily papers in Norway, the *Tidens Tegn* of Oslo, and was a man of means. He was assisted in this special business by Major Sverre and Secretary Bryn. There were a few members of the Aëro Club besides, but these three men pretty well monopolized the active enthusiasm as well as the offices of the organization. When I speak in this narrative of the Aëro Club of Norway, I am speaking, for all practical purposes, of these three individuals. They subsequently caused us troubles so numerous as to outweigh any services they rendered us. Indeed, most of the misunderstandings that have arisen in the public mind about the facts of the flight of 1926 are traceable directly to the mismanagement and weakness and vacillation of the Aëro Club of Norway.

These troubles began as early as January, 1926. In that month, Nobile went to Oslo to sign his contract as pilot of the expedition. As Ellsworth and I were in America, he dealt with the Aëro Club as our agents. After a discussion of terms, a contract was drawn up and both parties signed it. This contract included a provision that Nobile should receive for his work as pilot the sum of 40,000 kroner.

Again I interrupt my narrative to point out and emphasize this provision. Nobile, since the flight, has been trying to make it appear that he was equally, with Ellsworth and myself, responsible for the expedition, and that, like us, he was one of the unpaid leaders. The fact is, I repeat, that his contract of service with the expedition specified his salary and made him, as we had always intended, a hired employee.

The day after Nobile had signed this contract, he asked for another meeting with the Aëro Club, and there made an astonishing demand. He declared that he was already under contract for a flight in Japan during the same period which would be occupied by the flight of our expedition

118

RECEIVED AT 64 BROAD STREET, NEW YORK, AT————M. DATE———— DEC 30 1925
D 2253

LCM RV NW 868 OSLO 162   30 1150P PAGE 1/50
LINCOLN ELLSWORTH HOTEL AMBASSADORS NEWYORK
WILL FOLLOWING STATEMENT BE SATISFACTORY QUOTE IN ROALD
AMUNDSENS GREAT POLAR EXPEDITION WHICH WILL TAKE
PLACE NEXT SPRING IN THE DIRIGIBLE NORGE THE AMERICAN
EXPLORER LINCOLN ELLSWORTH KNOWN FROM HIS PARTICIPATION
IN AMUNDSENS LAST POLAR FLIGHT WILL PARTAKE AS A
LEADER WITH EQUAL RIGHTS AND

HANOVER 1811
TELEPHONE BROAD 5100   To secure prompt action on inquiries, this original RADIOGRAM should be presented at the office
of the Radio Corporation. In telephone inquiries guage the number preceding the place of origin

RECEIVED AT 64 BROAD STREET, NEW YORK, AT————M. DATE————192——
LCM RV NW868 LINDOLN PAGE 2/50
STANDING TO THOSE OF CAPTAIN AMUNDSEN STOP THE EXPEDITION
WILL BE CALLED THE AMUNDSEN ELLSWORTH TRANSPOLAR
FLIGHT 1926 STOP ITS RECORD WILL BE WRITTEN BY THE
TWO LEADERS IN COOPERATION STOP THE NORWEGIAN AERO-
CLUB IS IN CHARGE OF THE ADMINISTRATIVE MANAGEMENT OF
THE EXPEDITION WHICH WILL TAKE PLACE UNDER NORWEGIAN

HANOVER 1811
TELEPHONE BROAD 5100   To secure prompt action on inquiries, this original RADIOGRAM should be presented at the office
of the Radio Corporation. In telephone inquiries quote the number preceding the place of origin

FORM NO. 118 H

RECEIVED AT **64 BROAD STREET**, NEW YORK, AT———————M. DATE———————192——

LCM RV NW868 LINCOLN PAGE 3/62

COLOURS UNQUOTE PLEASE LET US KNOW IF YOU WISH ALTERATIONS
STOP STATEMENT WILL BE WIRED TO ALL LEADING NEWS AGENCIES
AND SENT TO LEADING GEOGRAPHICAL SOCIETIES STOP WE ALSO
PREPARE ARTICLE ABOUT PREPARATIONS PLANS EXPEDITION
TO BE PUBLISHED SHORTLY IN ALL CONTACTING NEWSPAPERS
AND WILL THERE MAKE PERFECTLY CLEAR THAT YOU ARE LEADER
ON EQUAL STANDING TO AMUNDSEN HAPPY NEW YEAR

THOMMESSEN

HANOVER 1811

TELEPHONE BROAD 5100   To secure prompt action on inquiries, this original RADIOGRAM should be presented at the office
of the Radio Corporation. In telephone inquiries quote the number preceding the place of origin.

This facsimile copy of a radiogram from Mr. Thommessen of the
Aëro Club of Norway, together with the two subsequent radiograms
reproduced on the page following, indicate fairly clearly that Mr.
Thommessen was under no misapprehension as to who were to be
the leaders of the Norge Expedition to the North Pole.

RADIOGRAM

WORLD WIDE WIRELESS
RADIO CORPORATION OF AMERICA
IN CONNECTION WITH
"STAVANGER RADIO"
"*Via* RCA"   SEN KONGELIG NORSK RIKSTELEGRAFSTYRET.   "*Via* RCA"

THE ONLY DIRECT TELEGRAPHIC
CONNECTION AMERICA-NORWAY.
          BEN ENESTE DIREKT TELEGRAF
FORBINDELSE AMERIKA-NORGE.

FORM No. 112 H

RECEIVED AT **64 BROAD STREET**, NEW YORK, AT————M. DATE————

C L   JAN 22 1926   11 07 AM

LCMWJ

NW 1423 OSLO 11 22 320PM

LINCOLN ELLSWORTH SAINTREGIS HOTEL NEWYORK   D 799

STATEMENT SENT LEADING GEOGRAPHICAL SOCIETIES

THOMMESSEN

FOR MESSENGER
CALL COLUMBUS 4311
4312
1824 BROADWAY
NEAR COLUMBUS CIRCLE

HANOVER 1811

TELEPHONE: BROAD 5100   To secure prompt action on inquiries, this original RADIOGRAM should be presented at the office of the Radio Corporation. In telephone inquiries quote the number preceding the place of origin

RADIOGRAM

WORLD WIDE WIRELESS
CONTINENT TO CONTINENT   SHORE TO SHIP   SHIP TO SHIP

"*Via* RCA"   RADIO CORPORATION OF AMERICA   "*Via* RCA"

FORM No. 112 B
RECEIVED AT   AT————M. DATE————102

FA86/D662/LCMNW1040

OSLO 24/22   C L   JAN 7 1926   11 36 AM

7 255P

LINCOLN ELLSWORTH HOTEL AMBASSADORS NY (DELIVER 603 PARK AVE)

STATEMENT CABLED ASSOCIATED PRESS UNITED PRESS CONSOLIDATED PRESS

NORTH AMERICAN NEWSPAPERALLIANCE AND GREAT EUROPEAN NEWSAGENCIES

TODAY

THOMMESSEN

FOR MESSENGER
CALL COLUMBUS 4311
4312
1824 BROADWAY
NEAR COLUMBUS CIRCLE

TELEPHONE: To secure prompt action on inquiries, this original RADIOGRAM should be presented at the office of the Radio Corporation. In telephone inquiries quote the number preceding the place of origin across the Arctic Ocean. To accompany us, he pointed out, meant that he would have to cancel his Japanese contract and lost the money it would have brought him. Of course, he must have known all this the day before, when he had set 40,000 kroner as his own remuneration and had signed the contract containing that provision. Now nevertheless, on the day following, he gave this Japanese contract as his reason for demanding an additional 15,000 kroner.

The Aëro Club at this point should certainly have showed its mettle. Anybody of strong character and ordinary good judgment would decisively have resented this proposal. How could they expect to preserve the discipline of the expedition if they weakly yielded to this impudent demand? I am even yet at a loss to imagine what Thommessen could have been thinking about, to knuckle under to this piece of brazen effrontery. But instead of meeting this issue with courage, he weakly gave in.

Naturally, Nobile followed up his advantage. Ellsworth in New York the next day received a radiogram from the Aëro Club, the original copy of which has been lost, but a true copy of which, supplied by the Radio Corporation of America, reads as follows:

WE ARE CONSIDERING CONTRACT WITH NOBILE WHO VERY KEEN ON WRITING TECHNICAL PART OF POLAR BOOK STOP HE AGREES HOWEVER FOLLOWING PARAGRAPH QUOTE THE FINAL ACCOUNT OF THE EXPEDITION IS TO BE COMPILED BY AMUNDSEN AND ELLSWORTH IN CONNECTION WITH THOSE WHOM THEY MAY CHOOSE AS COLLABORATORS STOP IT IS UNDERSTOOD THAT NOBILE IN THIS QUALITY WILL UNDERTAKE TO COMPILE AND PREPARE THE PART OF THE WORK CONTAINING THE PREPARATION MANOUERING [MANOEUVRING] AND NAVIGATION OF THE

RADIOGRAM

WORLD WIDE WIRELESS
RADIO CORPORATION OF AMERICA
IN CONNECTION WITH
"STAVANGER RADIO"

Via RCA   *Via RCA*

THE ONLY DIRECT TELEGRAPHIC
CONNECTION AMERICA – NORWAY.   DEN KONGELIG NORSK RIKSTELEGRAFSTYRET.   DEN ENESTE DIREKT TELEGRAF
FORBINDELSE AMERIKA – NORGE.

FORM NO. 112 N

RECEIVED AT 64 BROAD STREET, NEW YORK. AT 1926 JAN 15 AM 1048 STANDARD TIME

LCMMJ

NW 1494   OSLO 111 15 16 PAGE ONE 50   D 800

LINCOLN ELLSWORTH SAINTREGIS HOTEL NEWYORK

WE ARE CONSIDERING CONTRACT WITH NOBILE WHO VERY KEEN

ON WRITING TECHNICAL PART OF POLAR BOOK STOP HE AGREES

HOWEVER FOLLOWING PARAGRAPH QUOTE THE FINAL ACCOUNT OF

THE EXPEDITION IS TO BE COMPILED BY AMUNDSEN AND ELLSWORTH

INCONNECTION WITH THOSE WHOM THEY MAY CHOOSE

TELEPHONE: HANOVER 1811   To secure prompt action on inquiries, this original RADIOGRAM should be presented at the office of the Radio Corporation. In telephone inquiries quote the number preceding the place of origin.

RADIOGRAM

WORLD WIDE WIRELESS
RADIO CORPORATION OF AMERICA
IN CONNECTION WITH
"STAVANGER RADIO"

Via RCA   *Via RCA*

THE ONLY DIRECT TELEGRAPHIC
CONNECTION AMERICA – NORWAY.   DEN KONGELIG NORSK RIKSTELEGRAFSTYRET.   DEN ENESTE DIREKT TELEGRAF
FORBINDELSE AMERIKA – NORGE.

FORM NO. 112 N

RECEIVED AT 64 BROAD STREET, NEW YORK. AT _____ STANDARD TIME

LCMMJ

NW 1494 LIN PAGE 2ND 61   D 800

AS COLLABORATORS STOP IT IS UNDERSTOOD THAT NOBILE IN

THIS QUALITY WILL UNDERTAKE TO COMPILE AND PREPARE THE

PART OF THE WORK CONTAINING THE PREPARATION MANOUERING

AND NAVIGATION OF THE AIRSHIP UNQUOTE STOP HOPE YOU CAN

ACCEPT THIS AS NOBILE UNDERSTAND WELL THAT HE IS TO

LIMIT HIS WORK TO THE AERONAUTICE SIDE OF THE EXPEDITION

STOP THANKFUL FOR IMMEDIATE ANSWER

AEROCLUB

TELEPHONE: HANOVER 1811   To secure prompt action on inquiries, this original RADIOGRAM should be presented at the office of the Radio Corporation. In telephone inquiries quote the number preceding the place of origin.

Facsimile of radiogram referred to on the previous page

AIRSHIP UNQUOTE STOP HOPE YOU CAN ACCEPT THIS AS NOBILE UNDERSTAND WELL THAT HE IS TO LIMIT HIS WORK TO THE AERONAUTICE SIDE OF THE EXPEDITION STOP THANKFUL FOR IMMEDIATE ANSWER

(signed) AEROCLUB

Ellsworth obeyed his first impulse and cabled in reply that he had no objection to this proposal. After acting upon that impulse, however, he decided to call on the then Norwegian Minister to the United States, who happened to be visiting in New York and was stopping at the Plaza Hotel. This was His Excellency, F. Herman Gade, who is now Norwegian Minister to Brazil and temporarily stationed in Washington, D. C., on a special mission to the American government from Norway. Mr Gade warned Ellsworth of the danger of permitting Nobile to write anything at all about the expedition and strongly advised him to recall his consent.

Facsimile of radiogram referred to on the opposite page

Ellsworth at once acted on Gade's advice and cabled the Aëro Club to hold up the matter of Nobile's request until he and I should reach Oslo. Four days later he got a reply which read:

SORRY BUT CONTRACT NOBILE SIGNED AFTER RECEIVING YOUR CABLE SIXTEENTH.

It is important at this point again to emphasize the fact that the Aëro Club's cable referred only to a *technical* chapter in the book. Neither Ellsworth nor I would have objected to such a chapter. Months later, after the flight had been completed, we learned that Thommessen had permitted Nobile to add the words "and aeronautical" to the word "technical" – an addition of which we were never informed and to which we would never have assented. The reader should keep clearly in mind throughout this narrative a thing that was always perfectly clear in my mind and Ellsworth's, namely, that we regarded Nobile solely as a paid employee, and that at no stage of the preparations nor during the flight did we ever consent that he should be regarded otherwise, with one sole exception which will appear a little later. Certainly, we never intended and did not consent to his sharing in any financial returns from the expedition. Our money had paid for the expedition, including the payment of a salary to Nobile. If there were to be any financial returns, as from a book or other writings, certainly we had no reason to share these returns with Nobile. The 55,000 kroner were ample compensation for his efforts. Nobile's later appearance with newspaper articles and lectures, and his demand to be permitted to sign with us the newspaper articles which we wrote, were all things never intended by us and not possibly to be conceived as within his rights except by stretching beyond the bounds of plausibility the meaning of the words "and aeronautical" that were added to the contract without our knowledge.

Conclusive proof of the foregoing statements is found supplied by the text of our contract with the *New York Times* for the publication of the exclusive news, feature stories, and photographs relating to the expedition. This contract was signed by Mr Ellsworth on October 27, 1925. It is printed here in full in small type – not with the idea that the reader will care to peruse it in detail, but that he may do so if he wishes, and confirm from it the statements made above. He will observe that no mention whatever is made of Nobile, and that Ellsworth and I reserve to ourselves the exclusive use of all the literary material coming from the expedition:

October 27, 1925.

THE NEW YORK TIMES COMPANY
Times Annex
229 West 43d Street
New York City, N. Y.

DEAR SIRS:

Roald Amundsen of Norway and Lincoln Ellsworth of the United States have decided to make a transpolar airship flight during the year 1926 and are now making preparations therefor. In connection therewith they desire to sell the news, feature stories and photographs relating to the said Expedition and have conferred the rights to effect such sale on the undersigned Aëro Club.

We therefore for ourselves and on behalf of Roald Amundsen and Lincoln Ellsworth, whose signatures we undertake to procure to this letter, offer to sell to you the exclusive newspaper and magazine publication rights in and for North America and South America and covering all news, special articles and photographs descriptive of or dealing with all phases of the said Expedition, its preparatory stages, actual flight, progress, discoveries and results on the terms and conditions hereafter stated. We undertake specifically to deliver or cause to be delivered to you all material herein offered to you at such times, in such manner and so protected as to insure to you the first publication of each and every part thereof in the Western Hemisphere. Any details relating to the manner of transmission of the material to you in the course of the Expedition shall, so far as necessary, be arranged hereafter with your cooperation so as to give complete effect to this undertaking.

We agree that all material tendered to you hereunder shall be safeguarded to the utmost, that no member of the Expedition or person associated therewith shall furnish any information or pictures to anyone other than yourselves and that we will use our every effort to prevent any person or persons other than those associated with the Expedition, and any newspaper, magazine or publication in the Western Hemisphere from securing any information or material relating to any phase of the said Expedition.

It is contemplated that the airship will fly from Rome, Italy, to Spitzbergen, Norway, before hopping off for the transpolar flight. You shall have the right, without cost to you, to have your representative carried on the airship from Rome to Spitzbergen and every facility will be furnished him for transmission of such news or material as he may desire to send.

There shall be furnished to you prior to the actual flight at least three articles covering all phases relating to the preliminary stages of the Expedition to be signed alternately by Roald Amundsen and by Lincoln Ellsworth, and also news from time to time, by cable or radio, of the preparations for the flight. Cable and radio tolls to be paid by you. There shall be furnished you during the flight wherever and whenever communication is available, full radio or cable dispatches detailing the progress of the flight, signed by Roald Amundsen and Lincoln Ellsworth, and in the event of the incapacity of both by the acting leader of the Expedition. The tolls for such dispatches shall be paid by you. There shall be furnished you at the earliest possible time after the completion or termination of the flight (1) a detailed official narrative of the Expedition consisting of not less than twenty-five thousand (25,000) words to be signed by Roald Amundsen and Lincoln Ellsworth, or by either of them in the event of the incapacity of the other, or in the event of the incapacity of both, by any survivor of the flight, and (2) four feature articles of approximately three thousand (3,000) words each similarly signed so as fully to cover all phases of the Expedition.

You shall have the right, without further payment than below provided, to syndicate and resell in North America and South America any and all of the material covered by this letter, as well as the right to copyright all such material. No book shall be published by any member of the Expedition, whether of the land or air party, dealing with the Expedition or any of its phases, in whole or in part, until the expiration of one month after the publication by you of the last feature story dealing with the completed flight. You agree not to delay needlessly publication of these articles.

All radio and cable messages transmitted direct from the Expedition to the American Continent shall be addressed to you and you are promptly to relay such messages to the undersigned Aëro Club by the most expeditious route. The tolls for the transmission from you to the undersigned Aëro Club shall be borne by the latter.

The consideration to be paid by you for the exclusive rights and the full material delivered to you, in accordance with the terms hereinabove stated, shall be the total sum of fifty-five thousand dollars ($55,000), payable nineteen thousand dollars ($I9,000) on the acceptance of this offer by you and the affixing of the signatures of Roald Amundsen and Lincoln Ellsworth to this letter, eighteen thousand dollars ($18,000) when you shall have been duly advised that the airship has reached Spitzbergen, Norway, and the balance of eighteen thousand dollars ($18,000) at the end of the Expedition, provided the Expedition shall have penetrated within approximately fifty miles of the North Pole and have explored hitherto unknown regions. In the event that the flight shall be terminated before reaching such point, the said last payment shall not be made and the total consideration shall be reduced to the sum of thirty-seven thousand dollars ($37,000), but the obligations to furnish the official narrative and the four feature articles on the termination of the flight, as hereinabove provided, shall, nevertheless, continue in full force and effect.

Your acceptance of the foregoing, noted at the foot hereof, shall, when the signatures of Roald Amundsen and Lincoln Ellsworth are affixed hereto, constitute a contract between us.

Very truly yours,

We hereby accept the foregoing.
NEW YORK TIMES COMPANY
By
By
(Under annexed Power of Attorney)

In March, 1926, Ellsworth and I arrived in Oslo and from there made our way to Rome to take over the *N-1* from the Italian government. We had to change cars in Berlin, and it so happened that we had thirteen minutes in which to get from one train to another in order to take the Rome express. As we alighted from the first train, a telegram was thrust into my hands. It was signed by Thommessen's secretary and asked me to telephone back to Oslo, because Nobile had just informed the Aëro Club that the Italian government would not give us possession of the ship until $15,000 of insurance money had been paid. I cannot imagine where the Club got the idea that I could, in thirteen minutes, improvise a solution of this wholly unexpected problem, besides getting a telephone connection through from Berlin to Oslo before taking the Rome express. Naturally, I let the matter go until we got to Rome.

When we arrived at Rome, we went into conference with Thommessen, the president of the Aëro Club of Norway, who had preceded us there. It quickly became apparent that Thommessen had lost his head completely. Whatever the Italians wanted done, Thommessen was even more eager than they to do. I have never been able to determine whether the Italians had flattered him out of his self-possession or whether the prospect of an Italian decoration, which he later got, had destroyed his sense of proportion; in any event, he appeared to be considering only the wishes of the Italians and to think very little either of the pride of Norway or Ellsworth's and my interests, which he was supposed to represent.

First of all, Thommessen presented to Ellsworth and me a fresh proposal from Nobile. This was that we should add Nobile's name to the designation of the expedition, so that it should be called the Amundsen-Ellsworth-Nobile Polar Expedition. We could see no sense in this proposal and immediately rejected it. Thommessen, however, pressed the point with great insistence. He explained that Italian local pride was running high, and he greatly feared, unless we made some concession to it, that means would be found to hinder us from getting possession of the *N-1*. He assured me further that the addition of Nobile's name was to be made only in compliment to Italy, and that it would never be heard of outside that country. The world already knew of the undertaking under its proper name of the Amundsen-

Ellsworth Expedition. No publicity would be given to Nobile after we got the *N-1* out of Italy, and no one would be deceived. Meanwhile, we should gratify local pride while we were taking the ship over. On these representations, we consented to add Nobile's name. We did not consent, neither would we ever have consented, to include him as having a share in the command, for reasons sufficiently explained above.

Thommessen's next point was a request for the money for the insurance of the dirigible. This, we agreed, was a perfectly reasonable demand. The *N-1* had to fly from Rome to Spitzbergen, and on this flight she had, of course, to be insured. We did not even quarrel with the fact that the $15,000 mentioned as the amount due in the telegram from Thommessen's secretary, now appeared to be $20,000. Ellsworth agreed to cable to America for the money, which should be considered as a loan to the Aëro Club of Norway. I should say, in passing, that the Club not only represented our financial interests but also was to share in a small percentage of any financial returns.

Now Thommessen made a final proposal. He asked if Ellsworth and I would call on Nobile. At this preposterous suggestion, I lost control of my patience. With great indignation, we inquired of Thommessen if he had lost his senses completely. Ellsworth and I were the commanders of the expedition, and Nobile was to be the hired pilot of a ship bought with Ellsworth's and my money. It was all very well to gratify local Italian pride by temporarily adding Nobile's name to ours in the title of the expedition, but I intended to have no misunderstanding as to Nobile's true status, and I certainly had no intention of putting myself in the absurd position of making a formal first call on a hired subordinate. Naturally, that ultimatum closed that subject. Nobile later paid his call.

Meanwhile, I had been holding conferences with the Norwegians whom I had selected as members of the expedition. They had been in Italy for some time to take part in the trial flights of the *N-I* before she should be delivered to us. Now I began to hear a lot of things that made me very angry. The tension between the Norwegian crew on the one side and Thommessen, Sverre, and Nobile on the other side was at the bursting point.

Worse things yet now came to light. When Nobile called on me, he at once started demanding all sorts of absurd concessions. First of all, he wanted the Norwegian, as well as the Italian members of the crew, to take an oath of personal allegiance to him. I rejected this insolent suggestion with indignation and emphatically pointed out to Nobile in plain terms that he was nothing but a hired pilot.

For the benefit of the non-nautical reader, I should here explain the distinction between the captain of a vessel and the commander of an expedition. This distinction applies equally whether the craft be a ship in the water or a ship in the air. The captain of a ship necessarily has to be in supreme command of its physical operation. A crew cannot take orders from two different men. Therefore, all orders for the handling of a ship must come from the captain. He is solely and absolutely responsible for every detail of its physical management while in motion. Helmsman and engineer and crew must respond to the direction of a single mind and will.

All the foregoing, however, relates solely to the physical management of the vessel. On an exploring I expedition, where the vessel shall go is absolutely within the province of the commander. He defines the objectives, and the captain of the vessel carries the commander's orders into effect by so ordering the management of the ship as to make it proceed safely to the point designated by the commander.

It was this sharp distinction between the functions of the skipper of the *N-1* and the commanders of the Polar expedition – Nobile being the former and myself and

Ellsworth the latter – which Nobile either could not, or would not, get into his head. The demands he made were efforts to usurp our function as commanders. Our responses to these demands were uniformly and emphatically and explicitly negative.

The foregoing will explain Nobile's next demand and my answer. Nobile wanted to stipulate that if, in his judgment, when we got to the North Pole, the air conditions were unfavourable to continue the flight southward to our objective, Point Barrow, he should be at liberty to turn the *N-1* back and return to Spitzbergen. To this request I responded with a blunt and emphatic "nothing doing." We explained again to Nobile that his sole function was skipper of the ship. Our function was command of the expedition, and our orders as to where the ship should go must be unquestioningly accepted.

"Then," pleaded Nobile, "will you consult my opinion?"

"Certainly," we answered; "we should be very stupid if we did not get the skipper's expert opinion of what he could do with his ship before making any decision."

Nevertheless, we would make the final decision and he would have to abide by it. We also explained to him again that we were not interested in getting to the North Pole – that the whole object of our expedition was to make the continent-to-continent flight across the Arctic Ocean – and that nothing short of obvious inability to complete that flight would have the slightest influence in persuading us to turn back at any point along the course. Nobile then asked for a repeated assurance that he would be consulted, asking that any final decision we should make should be after a conference of four of us, namely, myself and Ellsworth, Nobile and Riiser-Larsen. As these were obviously the four people I should certainly consult in any event, I had no hesitation in answering "yes."

In the light of what has since happened, it is now clear enough that Nobile, in all of these manoeuvres, was trying desperately to insinuate himself into a position of major command of the expedition. Later events on the flight convinced me that this was not merely the product of Nobile's personal vanity and ambition – though these were great enough, in all conscience. I became pretty well convinced that he was also acting under orders from the government. They saw an opportunity to seize the credit for our exploit as an Italian achievement, and they used every device to attain this end. What some of these schemes were will appear a little later.

Finally came the great day for us formally to take over the dirigible from the Italians. The *N-1* was now officially renamed the *Norge.* Naturally, I had insisted not only that the ship should fly the Norwegian flag, but also that she should bear the name of my country. The Italians made the event literally "a Roman holiday." Thommessen took over the ship. The Italian colours were lowered and the Norwegian hoisted. Without our knowledge, the Aëro Club had given permission also that the ship should bear her old name, *N-1,* as well as her new name *Norge,* and at the same time had agreed that the Italian colours should be painted on the hull.

On March 29th, the *Norge* took the air and travelled north.

Ellsworth and I immediately returned to Oslo by train. Neither of us had the slightest interest in the celebrations that we knew would mark the *Norge's* progress from Rome to Spitzbergen. It would be at best an uncomfortable trip. Ellsworth and I were in for the trip over the unknown – we were not interested in seeing European scenery from the air or in meeting crowds in England, Germany, and Russia. Besides, we had important preparations to continue in Norway and naturally we hastened there as fast as possible.

Nobile has of late declared that this flight from Rome to Spitzbergen was far more dangerous than the one from Spitzbergen to Point Barrow. Even the most uninitiated reader can surmise how silly this claim is. The *Norge* had made hundreds of flights over various parts of Europe before we took her over. She was piloted through France by an experienced French pilot; over the English Channel, England, and the North Sea by an experienced English pilot. The journey was a perfectly safe one. For Ellsworth and me to have made it would have been to waste our time.

Safe as the journey was, Nobile grossly mismanaged even that. Besides the necessary foreign pilots taken aboard at Rome to guide the *Norge* over other lands, Nobile permitted on board a large number of newspaper correspondents, and guests who travelled for the mere notoriety of the experience. One result was discomfort for everybody on board. Another result was the wholly needless discomfort of the Norwegian members of the expedition – Riiser-Larsen, Omdal, and the others of my boys. My old friend Dr Adam of Berlin had generously made flying suits to measure for every member of the expedition. These suits were skillfully made, with a knowledge of the bitter weather to be encountered in the north. They were as light as was possible and yet as warm as was necessary. Dr Adam shipped these suits to Rome in ample time to arrive before the *Norge* started. They were on the ground ready to be used. At the last moment, Nobile declared they could not be carried because of their weight. Riiser-Larsen, therefore, and the other Norwegians had to make the flight from Rome to Spitzbergen clad in ordinary street clothes. The Italians, however, when the *Norge was* ready to rise at Rome, appeared on the scene clad in magnificent fur coats and equipped with every other comfort of apparel. Throughout the journey the Norwegians suffered intensely from the cold. Even Riiser-Larsen, rugged giant that he is and bred to the Northern climate, arrived in Spitzbergen with his teeth chattering. The whole incident was an exhibition of brutal lack of consideration on Nobile's part. There was no reason in the world why the Norwegians should not have been allowed to wear their suits. Nobile himself and his Italian comrades were supplied. The suits for all the Norwegians combined certainly weighed less than the weight of one man. Nobile carried several unnecessary passengers on the flight, any one of whom could easily have been left behind. The incident was of a piece with Nobile's treatment of Riiser-Larsen and the rest during the trial flight in Italy. His arrogance and egotism and selfishness were unparalleled in my experience. I shall have later incidents of the same kind to report in this narrative.

Ellsworth and I finished our business at Oslo and proceeded on to Spitzbergen before the *Norge* reached Oslo. Here again we were not concerned about the demonstrations of the crowd. There were preparations to be made at Spitzbergen, and our duty was to be there making them in advance of the *Norge's* arrival. We reached Spitzbergen on April 13th. The *Norge* arrived May 7th.

We had rented ground on Kings Bay, Spitzbergen, from a Norwegian coal company which operates a mine there. The coal company had built a quay for its vessels and a railroad from the quay out to the mine – a distance of about a mile. The Aëro Club had had a crew of men working near this mine the whole winter, erecting a sort of hangar. This hangar did not have a roof. It was really a three-sided windbreak and a very useful device, though, of course, not as ideal as it would have been with a roof. Our first task when we arrived at Spitzbergen was to clear the snow off the railroad track from the quay to the hangar. As the snow was about six to nine feet deep, this was a somewhat difficult job.

While these preparations were proceeding, the *Norge* had reached Gatschina, where she stayed until everything should be ready for her in Spitzbergen.

Both here in Spitzbergen, and in Oslo while on the way thither, Ellsworth and I had encountered further evidences of the Aëro Club's mismanagement. There were bills for trips to Rome made by Thommessen, Sverre, and Bryn. What these were for, we could not determine. Nevertheless, they had been made and the expedition was expected to pay for them. While we were in Spitzbergen, the Aëro Club asked Ellsworth for another $10,000. He and I were now so utterly disgusted that we considered throwing up the whole expedition. Only the fear that someone else would follow out our plans and accomplish the feat before we should have time to organize another expedition prevented us from taking this drastic step.

At length, everything was ready and the *Norge* proceeded to Spitzbergen by way of Vadso, arriving at her final destination on May 7th. She was safely housed in the hangar, and everybody went busily to work making ready for the flight. Provisions and fuel must be taken on, and it developed that one of the motors had to be replaced. This work occupied us for five days. During that time the Italians spent their odd hours practicing on skis. I should not bother to record so minor a detail were it not for the silly claims that Nobile is now making to a major share in the expedition and to the credit for a share in the conception of the enterprise. If anyone before this had ever supposed that these Italians had seriously thought of Polar exploration until they had an opportunity to go with experienced Arctic workers, the exhibition they gave on the ice would have been sufficient to settle the question. They were unbelievably clumsy. None of them could stay on their feet more than a few moments. I remember on one occasion Nobile fell on smooth ground and could not get up, so that he had to be assisted to his feet. It is merely amusing to suppose that men of this semi-tropical race, who had not the most rudimentary idea of how to take care of themselves in a cold country, could ever have conceived the notion of undertaking on their own account an expedition which required as its most elementary qualification an ability to survive on the ice in an emergency.

Indeed, before the *Norge* left Italy, Nobile took Riiser-Larsen to one side and made him promise "if we have to get down on the ice you will not leave us Italians and save yourselves." That the man who now has the effrontery to try to belittle the parts played by Ellsworth and myself and my Norwegian compatriots in this expedition – that this man had let the thought even enter his head that men of our past record could be so base that he would need such a reassurance, only reveals his own mind! Before I go any farther, I want to speak of the five other Italians on the expedition. These five subordinates were fine fellows. They were skilled in their several occupations. They performed their duties cheerfully and efficiently. They were always good comrades. We liked them all. They made no pretense to be other than they were. Wherever in this narrative I may speak in criticism of the Italian contingent on the expedition, I mean Nobile specifically and only.

A few days before the *Norge* arrived at Spitzbergen, Commander Richard E. Byrd of the United States Navy arrived on his ship *Chantier.* A lot of misrepresentations about our attitude toward Byrd's expedition have been foisted on the public mind by unfriendly correspondents. I shall, therefore, take this opportunity to describe in some detail exactly what happened and why. So far as Commander Byrd himself is concerned, this explanation is quite unnecessary. He fully understood the reasons for everything that happened, and he and I were then and still are on terms of the most cordial friendship and mutual understanding.

The quay which I have already described was the only facility at Kings Bay for discharging cargo from a vessel.

It was so short that only one vessel could be tied to it at a time. When the *Chantier* arrived, that space was occupied by the *Heimdal,* the vessel which had brought some of the men to Spitzbergen. The *Heimdal* was at the moment taking on coal and water. More important than this, however, she was engaged in making essential repairs to her boiler, which was out of order. And most important of all, the *Norge* would soon be on her way from Gatschina to Spitzbergen, and the captain of the *Heimdal* must be ready at this time to come to her assistance if such be needed. For these reasons, it was impossible for the *Heimdal* to move away from the quay to anchorage in order to make room for the *Chantier* to tie up and unload.

It would be only a few days before this could be done, but Byrd was not willing to wait. Quite naturally, he was all keyed up to start on his flight to the North Pole, and he chafed at the thought of being delayed even for a few days. He therefore undertook to land his two airplanes from the *Chantier's* anchorage. He resorted to a daring expedient, which was executed with amazing speed and skill. Under his direction a pontoon was constructed by lashing four small boats together. Boards were laid across their gunwales to make a platform. The 'planes were lowered on to this deck and the pontoon was towed through the floating ice to the shore. It was a very risky business, but its success was as brilliant as its conception.

Ignorant critics have tried to make the public believe that our expedition purposely hampered Byrd's landing. Their theory is that we were jealous of the prospect that he would beat us to the Pole. The reader by now must be fully aware that the Pole was not our objective. Byrd himself was aware of that fact, for in New York, six weeks earlier, I had talked personally with him and had said to him: "We do not count you as a competitor, as we are not interested in the Pole." Our objective was Alaska, and the Pole was only an interesting incident. Byrd's whole idea was something entirely different. His sole purpose in his flight was to reach the Pole and return without landing. Never at any stage of the proceedings has there been or is there any rivalry or jealousy between us.

Nobile, however, when he arrived a few days later with the *Norge,* took a different attitude. This was not surprising in view of his previous efforts to persuade me to permit him to turn back once the *Norge* reached the Pole. Evidently this notion, so alien to my own intention on the expedition, still persisted in his mind. As soon as he had got the *Norge* into the hangar after his arrival and had heard that Byrd had landed his 'planes on the beach and was concluding his preparations for his flight, Nobile came to me and said: "The *Norge* can be ready in three days."

I instantly responded: "Nothing doing. We are not running a race with Byrd to the North Pole. I do not care in the slightest whether he reaches it ahead of us or not. Our job is to cross the Arctic Ocean."

In keeping with this consistent purpose, and wishing Byrd all the luck in the world, I gladly shared, with him the use of the land at Kings Bay which we had leased from the coal company. We bade him god-speed and gave him a cheer when he started. On his return, sixteen to seventeen hours later, I was at dinner. Someone at the table remarked that, if Byrd was to have the good fortune to get back, it was about time he was returning: The words were hardly out of his mouth when we heard the hum of his motor. We leaped from our chairs and left our unfinished dinner. We led the dash up to the place where he would land: It so happened that Byrd's own comrades were also at dinner aboard the *Chantier* at her anchorage. It thus so happened that Ellsworth, I, and our Norwegians formed the majority of those at the landing place to greet Byrd and Bennett when their 'plane came to rest and they dismounted. We had caught up motion-picture cameras as we ran out, and the only pictures of Byrd's triumphant safe return are the ones we took. I was one of the first to shake Byrd's hand as he stepped out of his 'plane and to congratulate him whole-heartedly on the success of his flight. I then turned to my companions and called on them to "give nine good Norwegian cheers" for Byrd and Bennett, which they did with a will!

Commander Byrd cannot be too highly praised for his flight. He and his pilot, Floyd Bennett, deserve the highest admiration for their courage – few more hazardous ventures have ever been undertaken in history. To say nothing of the practical certainty of death if they had been forced to land and had been unable to rise again, the dangers of the flight were multiplied by the difficulties involved in making accurate observations of position in those regions. The magnetic compass is there very sluggish, and even if it were accurate in those latitudes, still the difficulties of making accurate observations in a 'plane travelling a hundred miles an hour would have made the work of the navigator extremely difficult. If considered only as a feat of navigation, Commander Byrd's exploit is one of the most remarkable on record.

On the evening of May 10th, everything was ready for the *Norge* to start. We had a conference that evening and agreed to leave at one o'clock in the morning. I should remind the reader that at this season of the year in the Arctic the sun never sets. At 1 a.m., however, it would be at its lowest point on the horizon. The air at that hour would consequently be at its coldest. The gas in the balloon attains its greatest lifting capacity at the lowest temperature. That was the reason this hour was chosen.

I was wakened about midnight by the watchman, who explained that a wind had sprung up and that our start would be delayed. I went back to sleep and was wakened again at six o'clock by a man who brought the message that everything now was all right. I got up and had breakfast and went up to the hangar. Word was brought us that, on account of the wind and the consequent difficulty in manoeuvring the dirigible, we should bring with us as little as possible of personal effects. Ellsworth and I, therefore, went up to the hangar with only what we had on.

Imagine our astonishment to find everything about the airship in confusion. Men were running hither and yon, carrying packages aboard the gondolas. Nobile was standing off to one side, apparently in a state of equal confusion. When we came up, he explained to us that the sun had now risen so far that it had touched the top of the gas bag, the gas had expanded, and he did not venture to start. Ellsworth and I went on up to the hangar. Suddenly, someone came running up, calling: "We're off." Puzzled to know the reason for this sudden change of front, but assuming, of course, that it had some reason, Ellsworth and I went aboard, and in a few moments we were in the air.

Later, we learned what had happened. Riiser-Larsen had come up to Nobile after we had left him, and found Nobile in such a state of nervous excitement as to be incapable of action. Nobile had cried out that he would not be responsible for what would happen if the *Norge* were brought out of the hangar into the wind. Riiser-Larsen made a contemptuous retort that the little breeze then blowing was a matter of no moment. Thereupon Nobile threw up his hands and exclaimed:

"If you will take the responsibility, then take her out of the hangar."

Riiser-Larsen had thereupon accepted the responsibility, and with the assistance of Lieutenant Hover the final swift preparations were made under his orders. The moving pictures, taken of these last moments when the *Norge* was brought out of the hangar and we took the air, show Riiser-

Larsen giving the orders and Nobile standing fatuously to one side, doing nothing. Here again Nobile demonstrated his conduct in an emergency. We were to have yet further demonstrations on the flight.

The *Norge* took the air on her epoch-making journey from Spitzbergen at ten o'clock in the morning (local time) on May 11, 1926.

Forty-two hours later, we sighted Point Barrow on the north coast of Alaska. My dream of years had come true! My career as an explorer had been crowned with success in practically the last of the great possible achievements. We had crossed the Arctic Ocean from continent to continent.

The distance travelled by the *Norge* had been estimated at 3,391 miles. The distance in a right line from Spitzbergen to Point Barrow is about 2,200 miles; from there to Teller about 1,000 miles more. Too high praise cannot be given Riiser-Larsen, who did all the work of navigation. So skillfully did he chart our course that, after this prodigiously long flight – longer than an air route from New York to San Diego – over unbroken fields of unexplored ice, with not a single landmark for a guide, we sighted Point Barrow with a total deviation from our objective of not more than ten miles.

This is not all the credit that belongs to Riiser-Larsen. Three times on the flight his presence of mind saved us from disasters into which Nobile's nervousness and utter lack of self-control threatened to plunge us. These incidents belong with those I have mentioned before, as the kind of thing men try to forget and not to mention when the trials of an expedition are over. I should not discuss them now were it not that Nobile has brazenly tried to claim, not only the honours of a pilot, which was his only function, but also major honours of the expedition itself. Otherwise, I should not take the trouble to show, by the following incidents, that he was not equal even to the task of pilot.

To make these incidents clear to the reader, I must explain something of the construction and management of the *Norge*. Beneath her semi-rigid gas bag were suspended four gondolas, of which one was at the rear and two were on the sides. These contained the motors which drove the propellers. The larger gondola was farther forward. It was an enclosed structure, built like a small house and divided by partitions into three tiny rooms. The room farthest forward, because of the clear view ahead, was the pilot house. Here was the steering wheel, controlling our direction to the right or left as we sped along. Here also was the wheel that controlled other rudders which preserved our horizontal position, or which at will tilted the airship upward or downward. And here finally were the levers controlling the gas valves. By manipulating these so as to release the gas from one chamber or another, or from all simultaneously, the pilot was able to control the equilibrium of the ship and its elevation. This last – the management of the gas bags – was Nobile's sole function as pilot.

Directly aft of this pilot room was a tiny room for the navigator and the rest of the crew. Here were instruments for taking observations, maps, and a table on which to work out calculations. This was Riiser-Larsen's and the whole crew's workshop. At best this space was crowded, for besides Nobile, Ellsworth, Riiser-Larsen, and myself, six members of the crew occupied this forward gondola. Six mechanics occupied the three smaller gondolas that housed the motors.

Nobile and I spent most of our time in the pilot's cabin. Naturally, I had the easiest task of all on board. The others did the work of keeping the ship going, and going to the right objective. My function was solely that of the explorer, watching the terrain below, studying its geographical character, and especially keeping an alert eye out for any signs of a possible Arctic continent.

Ellsworth was occupied a good part of the time taking observations to measure the atmospheric electricity of the regions through which we passed. These observations were made at the request of the Curie Institute of Paris, by means of a special machine lent us for the purpose. Ellsworth's original intention, when the expedition was first planned, was to help Riiser-Larsen calculate the navigation of the ship. He had preceded me to Norway by a month to take special studies to perfect himself in the art of navigation, with which he was already familiar. But when we got to Spitzbergen and found the organization was all set up, Ellsworth was too large spirited to interfere, and so devoted himself to his electrical observations and to such other useful things as he could find to do.

Naturally, Riiser-Larsen's whole time was not occupied by his calculations of our course. A good deal of his time was spent with Nobile and me in the pilot house, observing the instruments indicating our wind drift, and other technical devices that were related to his calculations. It was indeed fortunate for us all that Riiser-Larsen had to be a part of the time in the pilot house, as will appear when I now relate the three incidents alluded to above.

One of my comrades on the dash to the South Pole was also with me on the *Norge* flight. This was Oscar Wisting, one of the finest fellows that ever lived. Wisting was managing the vertical control in the pilot house – of course, under Nobile's supervision. Nobile asked Wisting to let him take the control so that he could get the "feel" of the balance of the ship. Wisting stood aside and Nobile took the control. Imagine my astonishment to see Nobile standing with his back to the nose of the ship while he turned the wheel around several times in a careless manner. The nose of the *Norge* responded and tilted downward toward the ice. As I was facing forward, I could see that we were getting closer and closer to the surface. I looked at Nobile and he seemed not to realize what was going on. He seemed, indeed, to be standing in a sort of daze. I said nothing. I would have said nothing if we had crashed, for I adhered throughout the voyage strictly to my status of commander and left the operation of the ship absolutely to Nobile as skipper, to whom, by the right of the sea and the right of the air, it belonged.

Riiser-Larsen, however, did not hold so strictly to the code. It was fortunate for us that he did not, else none of us would have come back to tell the tale. The ship was speeding swiftly toward the rough ice below us. Another moment, and we should be dashed to pieces. Riiser-Larsen sensed the danger. Nobile seemed insensible to it: he stood like a man in a trance. Riiser-Larsen sprang to the wheel himself, thrust Nobile roughly to one side, and himself spun the wheel around. So close was our call that we thrust our heads out of the cabin window to see if the rear motor could possibly clear the ice. Fortunately, it did, but it was a matter of inches.

Exactly this same incident happened a second time on the voyage, but with one variation. Again Riiser-Larsen saw us about to crash into the ice. This time he shouted a rough command of warning to Nobile to change our elevation. Nobile gave a start like a man coming out of a dream. Automatically, he obeyed Riiser-Larsen's command and whirled the wheel back a few revolutions. We barely cleared the ice as the *Norge,* responding to the rudder, rose again.

The third incident was this: Flying southward above the ice, the *Norge* ran into a heavy fog. This, of course, put us in an extremely dangerous position. Speeding along at fifty miles an hour, a slight downward deviation in the horizontal balance of our gas bag would be enough to send us headlong into the ice. Nobile at once did the only thing to do. He spun the wheel of the vertical control so as to point us upward in an effort to climb above the fog bank.

He was in such nervous haste to do this, however, that he gave no thought to the gas pressure in the bag. We mounted swiftly to a high altitude. Suddenly Nobile "came to." We had reached a point so high as to reduce the atmospheric pressure on the outside of the gas bag to a point where the gas pressure inside threatened to burst the bag. Nobile now made a frantic effort to get the nose of the *Norge* pointed downward. The ship did not respond to the rudder. Then Nobile lost his head completely. With tears streaming down his face, and wringing his hands, he stood screaming: "Run fast to the bow! Run fast to the bow!" Three of our Norwegians dashed forward on the runway under the bag, and by their weight forced the *Norge's* nose downward.

A fourth incident occurred on the flight which alone would disprove the claim Nobile is now making to a major prominence in the expedition. Again I shall have to give the reader a brief explanation in order to make this incident intelligible. Navigators use a term which they call "the line of position." This is a line, of infinite length, of which the navigator knows nothing but its direction. His ship may be at any point on this line, but the navigator cannot know at what point until, several hours later, a second observation provides him with a second "line of position." The point at which these two "lines of position" intersect locates his actual geographical position on the map.

Not until this second observation is taken and this point of intersection is ascertained, can the navigator know where he is, or what course to steer to reach his destination. In other words, "the line of position" tells nothing about the next step in navigation until it is supplemented with other data. All this, of course, belongs to the a, b, c, of the art of navigation.

On the last leg of our flight, when we knew by calculation that we must be approaching the north coast of Alaska, Nobile went into Riiser-Larsen's office and inquired how we were getting along in our progress toward our objective. Riiser-Larsen replied, "I have just determined our line of position." Taking up a pencil, he drew a straight line on the map, and said to Nobile, "We are now on this line." Nobile cheerfully rejoined: "Fine! Now set the course for Point Barrow!"

A child in the art of navigation would have known better than to make such an absurd remark. It was, of course, impossible to "set the course for Point Barrow" until further observations showed Riiser-Larsen at what point he was on "the line of position." Nobile, however, who now pretends to have been the presiding genius of the expedition, was so ignorant of the elementary facts of the art of navigation as to be able to make this silly remark.

I must at this point take notice also of some of the absurd stories that have been circulated in the Italian press since the flight. For one thing, those papers have declared that the Italians did all the work while the Norwegian members of the expedition slept. The truth is that, though no one on board did more than snatch a few hours of uneasy slumber now and then, the one member of the expedition who slept by far the most was Nobile himself. As for the work, I was the only idle person on the expedition. I was idle in the sense that I did not lift a finger to do any physical work. My job, as explained above, was to keep my eyes open and my wits alert. Geographical observation was my sole business. Certainly Ellsworth had enough to do with his electrical observations. Riiser-Larsen did all the work of navigation, and Wisting and Horgen of the Norwegians had complete charge of the steering apparatus. A few times Nobile took the wheel to test the balance of the ship, but on these occasions, as I have recounted above, he did so at the imminent peril of the lives of all of us. Captain Gottwaldt was in charge of the wireless station and Dr Malmgren in charge of the meteorological observations.

Another nonsensical story circulated by the Italian press is that the *Norge* expedition was so divided by ill feeling as to have the appearance of division into two armed camps. Nothing could be further from the truth. I have already described the amiable disposition of the five Italians other than Nobile, and the personal regard in which I held them, a regard shared by my companions. On the flight itself there was not a trace of anything to break the even surface of the most amicable relations. Even Riiser-Larsen's opportune interference when Nobile lost his head did not affect the general amiability. In the air and during the dangers of the flight over what was to him so strange and forbidding a landscape, Nobile was the soul of meekness and humility. Presumptuous as he was before we left Spitzbergen, and braggart as he has been since we landed in Alaska, he made no pretensions to greatness on the flight.

Doubtless, many times during those seventy-two hours, his mind reverted apprehensively to his shameless appeal to Riiser-Larsen that we should not desert him if the ship came down. This was, indeed, a becoming humility, for, if we had been forced to the ice – as three times we very nearly were through his lack of self-control in emergencies – his plight would have been a serious one indeed. Unable even to keep his feet beneath him on skis, and utterly inexperienced in the art of Arctic travel, his chances of ever getting back to civilization would have been slim. It would never have occurred to us to desert the Italians. We would have shared with them the effort to work our way back over the ice, but their inexperience would certainly have cost us our lives as well as theirs. They could not possibly have maintained a pace that would have given us a chance for our lives.

Not even certain incidents of the passage over the actual North Pole could destroy the friendly atmosphere of the expedition, though Nobile's conduct there gave Ellsworth and me every ground for extreme irritation. Time and again, in the preparations for the flight, Nobile had insisted upon everybody keeping down to the barest minimum the amount of effects of whatever description that should be taken on board. He was forever harping on this subject. The reader will recall the selfish arrogance into which this mania led Nobile on the flight from Rome to Spitzbergen how he refused to permit the Norwegians to wear their Arctic suits while he and the other Italians appeared on board in comfortable fur coats. We were now, in crossing the North Pole, to discover further evidence of Nobile's callous disregard of the sensibilities of others.

Ellsworth and I had each, of course, brought a flag to be dropped overboard as we crossed the Pole – Ellsworth the Stars and Stripes and I the national flag of Norway. In keeping with Nobile's injunctions, we had each brought a little flag not much larger than a pocket handkerchief. As we crossed the Pole, we threw these overboard and gave a cheer for our countries. Imagine our astonishment to see Nobile dropping overside not one, but armfuls, of flags. For a few moments the *Norge* looked like a circus wagon of the skies, with great banners of every shape and hue fluttering down around her. Nobile produced one really huge Italian flag. It was so large he had difficulty in getting it out of the cabin window. There the wind struck it and it stuck to the side of the gondola. Before he could disengage it we must have been five miles beyond the Pole. When it finally flew free, it hurtled back to the rear gondola and there for an instant it seemed that it would become entangled with the propeller and give us serious trouble. At length it fluttered free and sank swiftly to the surface of the ice below us.

Fortunately, I have a sense of humour, which I count one of my chief qualifications as an explorer. Dangers, hardships, irritations that otherwise would be almost too much to be endured, lose their sting before the saving grace of humour. Scornful as I was at Nobile's overreaching in this matter, irritated as I was by his selfishness and presumption, I could still be amused at his childish pleasure in feeling that he had "put something over" and had gained a greater honour for his country by the size and number of its flags deposited in the unseeing vastness of the Arctic. That a grown man and a military officer could have so little imagination as to measure the value of such a moment by the physical size of its symbols rather than by the depth of the sentiment behind it struck me as so grotesque that I laughed aloud.

There was another touch of ironic humour in the occasion which I did not realize until afterward. Nobile still boasts that he dropped overboard at the Pole the banner of the Aëro Club of Italy. He will not know until he reads these lines that one of the Norwegian boys discovered this banner among the baggage unloaded in Alaska after we had made our descent at Teller! Even the gods smiled at the fatuous colonel!

I leave to the reader to imagine, if he can, the thrill we got when our eyes first discerned the north coast of Alaska. On a closer approach, I soon began to make out the familiar landmarks of this coast which I had first passed twenty years before in the little *Gjoa*. Everything was running smoothly, so we determined to follow the coast line down past Bering Strait and on to Nome. This programme did not work out satisfactorily. We soon got into fog and lost our bearings. Once we probably were close under the Siberian coast. We proceeded eastward by dead reckoning to avoid the possible necessity of a descent into the waters of the Pacific. After several hours, the fog cleared, and below us on the coast of Alaska we saw a strange settlement. I say "strange." If the reader will glance at the map of the coast line between Nome and Bering Strait, he will perceive that the normal course for a seagoing ship avoids the deep indentation of the coast about midway between these points. As it developed later, our flight through the fog had taken us into this deep inlet. Not even I was familiar with either the coast line or the village that lay below us. Certainly, however, we had reached civilization. Perhaps this would be the best place to make a landing. I inquired of Nobile how much fuel he had left.

"Enough for seven hours' flying," was his reply. "Could we make a landing here?" I asked. To this question he replied in the affirmative.

We then decided that all be made ready for landing. Warned, however, by previous experiences on the flight that Nobile's judgment was none of the best, I turned to Riiser-Larsen and asked him his opinion. His reply was that it was a safe place to land unless the wind should prove to be so heavy as to make the ship difficult to manage as we came near to the earth. He added that he had been taught in England, where he had studied the art of dirigible flying, that this danger could be largely obviated by knocking out the sides of the cabins in the gondola, an expedient that made it possible, if the landing proved too violent, for all hands on board to jump clear and alight in safety. Nobile heard this very sensible suggestion but excitedly shouted that we could not do it. He has since declared that Riiser-Larsen was making a wild suggestion in a panic. I can bear witness that it was made with the utmost calmness.

By an unexpected bit of good fortune, as we descended, the wind died off completely and Nobile made an excellent landing without any difficulty. We had been seventy-two hours in the air.

Citizens of the settlement, of course, crowded around us. There was general jubilation, much handshaking, and many congratulations. We learned that the name of the settlement was Teller. At once we identified it as a village about ninety miles northwest of Nome.

Almost the first thing that I heard when I stepped from the gondola to the ground was a woman's voice calling out, "How do you do, Captain Amundsen !" I turned and recognized an acquaintance of previous years in Nome. "Where are we?" I called out to her. "Teller," she replied. "Won't you come and stay with us?"

It developed that she was the mistress of one of two small hotels in Teller, or roadhouses as they are called in Alaska. I gratefully accepted the invitation, which was extended to include my companions. We were, of course, too large a company to be sheltered in the one small house. Other invitations were extended, and one in particular to Riiser-Larsen. He left us and went with his host, who showed him into a pair of fine rooms, one of them facing the sea and the other the land, with a bathroom between them. Riiser-Larsen's host deposited his luggage in the room facing the sea which, to a Norseman would, naturally, be more desirable. His host asked Riiser-Larsen if he would not like to invite some other member of the company to share the other room with him. With his native good nature and kindliness, Riiser-Larsen bethought him of Nobile, whom he hunted up and invited to share this nice apartment. Nobile accepted the invitation. Riiser-Larsen pointed out the house to him and came on down to supper at the house where we were quartered.

Of course, we had a merry evening. We were all elated at the success of the expedition. One of our hosts produced cigars and a bottle of good whisky. This and an appetizing dinner put us thoroughly at peace with all the world. At ten o'clock we were still enjoying this temperate festival of good cheer. Then in came Nobile with a visage of vinegar sourness and his lips pouting like a child. He demanded something to eat and ate what was brought to him in morose silence. We did not realize until later that he had suddenly redeveloped the swelling sense of his own importance, and that he was brooding like a spoiled baby over the lack of precedence and attentions which he felt were due him. When, at midnight,

Riiser-Larsen went back to the other house to turn in for well-earned slumbers, he found that his guest, the gallant Italian, had taken a fancy to the room in which his host had placed Riiser-Larsen and had thereupon, without more ado, picked up Riiser-Larsen's luggage and not removed but thrown it helter-skelter into the other room, shut the door, and gone to bed.

The reader at this point should be reminded that I am not trying in this volume to give an orderly narrative of the *Norge* flight: that has been written by me in another volume. What I am doing here is telling the unpleasant truth about those things that ordinarily are not told. I am telling them solely because Nobile and the Italian press have made of a great achievement a controversial issue. They have claimed for the Italians credit that does not belong to them. They have misrepresented the facts and have caused and are causing me financial loss and personal embarrassment. This narrative is written to give the public the whole truth about the matter, so that Nobile's actual part in the expedition may be accurately presented in its proper perspective to the main achievement. This hired skipper of a Norwegian ship owned by an American and myself shall not be permitted to usurp honours that do not belong to him. This record is written to prevent it.

With the landing at Teller, the expedition, as such, was at an end. All that remained to be done was to dismantle the dirigible and pack the gas bag for shipment. This, of course, was the task of Nobile and the crew. There was nothing more for Ellsworth and me to do so far as the expedition was concerned. Our first duty, therefore, was to get to the New York Times as quickly as possible the first installment of our story of the flight in accordance with our contract as printed earlier in this chapter. Naturally, we were anxious to get personal messages out to the world. All of us, therefore, made our way to the Teller wireless station, which was the only means of communication with the outside. To the deep disappointment of all, the station was out of order and none of us could send messages. I asked Captain Gottwaldt to get the apparatus in working order, and he got the instrument going again in a couple of days. Meanwhile, Nobile was furious because he could not get his messages out at once. His irritation was perfectly natural, but he treated the episode with childish petulance, going about all day with gloomy brow and pouting lips, as if someone had done him a personal injury.

On the second day of our stay in Teller, there being nothing more for Ellsworth or me to do there, we rented a gasoline launch and proceeded on to Nome, leaving Riiser-Larsen in command. We took with us Wisting and Omdal, leaving the other Norwegian boys to help the Italians dismantle the *Norge* and to follow with them to Nome. When we reached Nome, Omdal took the motor boat back to Teller to bring out the other members of the expedition when they should be ready.

Ellsworth and I stayed in Nome for three weeks altogether. As soon as we arrived, we got off, by cable, to the New York Times, the first part of our story of the flight. Meanwhile, the wireless at Teller had got going, and Nobile began sending out press dispatches himself. This was in direct violation of all our past agreements and gave Ellsworth and myself such irritation that Ellsworth cabled the Aëro Club at Oslo to protest against Nobile's unauthorized literary ventures.

Meanwhile, Nobile resumed his presumptuous attitude toward us. He sent a letter to Ellsworth by boat from Teller to Nome, marking it "confidential," in which he retailed to Ellsworth what he called his "many troubles." Apparently, he thought that, by appealing to Ellsworth and adopting a conciliatory tone toward him, he might cause a division between Ellsworth and me which would split our common counsels in such a way as to favour his own efforts to claim a major share in the undertaking. This was not only an underhand way of gaining his ends, but also showed him up as an extremely bad judge of character. Ellsworth is not the sort of person that a wise man approaches with that sort of proposition. He is a gentleman as well as a loyal friend and a clean sportsman. Quite naturally, the first thing Ellsworth did was to show me Nobile's letter, which he properly resented.

Among the "many troubles" that Nobile listed in his letter, he complained especially of the fact "that you and Amundsen are signing the Times articles without including my signature." Where in the world he got the idea that he had anything to do with the *Times* articles was a mystery to Ellsworth and me. We two had signed the contract with the *Times,* which the reader has already seen, and Nobile, at no stage of the proceedings, had ever been considered in that connection.

On the other hand, Ellsworth and I had every reason to be irritated with Nobile for presuming to write anything at all for publication about the expedition. The only writing Nobile was authorized to do that we had ever heard anything about was the writing of a chapter on the technical aspects of the flight. Even this, the reader will recall, Ellsworth had tried to head off when Minister Gade had warned him of the possible danger of permitting it. The cable about it that Ellsworth had received from the Aëro Club explicitly limited the subject matter of that chapter to the *technical* aspects of the flight.

When Ellsworth showed me Nobile's letter from Teller, he and I held a mutual indignation meeting over Nobile's impudence in writing at all for the daily press. As a result of our discussion Ellsworth cabled the Aëro Club at Oslo, as mentioned above, demanding an explanation.

Imagine our astonishment and anger upon receiving the following cablegram from the three responsible officers of the Aëro Club:

Form 1 2 8

SIGNAL CORPS, UNITED STATES ARMY
WASHINGTON-ALASKA MILITARY CABLE AND TELEGRAPH SYSTEM

TELEGRAM

RECEIVED at

20WXP J 209 VIA RCA POST
OSLO MAY 31 1926
LCD LINCOLN ELLSWORTH
NOME ALS
CONTRACT WITH NOBILE SIGNED IN PRESENCE OF RIISER LARSEN·AS REPRESENTATIVE
YOU AND AMUNDSEN HAS FOLLOWING ARTICLE QUOTE THE FINAL ACCOUNT OF THE
EXPEDITION IS TO BE COMPILED BY AMUNDSEN ELLSWORTH AND NOBILE IN CONNECTION
WITH THOSE WHOM THEY MAY CHOOSE AS COLLABORATORS STOP IT IS UNDERSTOOD
THAT NOBILE WILL COMPILE THE TECHNICAL AND AERONAUTICAL PART OF THE WORK
UNQUOTE THIS IS THE ONLY EXISTING PARAGRAPH CONCERNING PUBLICATION AND
SEEN IN CONNECTION WITH FACT THAT NOBILE HAS ALREADY WRITTEN ARTICLE
FOR PUBLICATION PRESS BEFORE DEPARTURE WE CONSIDER UNWISE AND BAD TASTE
OBJECT TO NOBILES RIGHT COLLABORATION STOP GENERAL DISCONTENT CONTRACTING
NEWS PAPERS DUE TO SMALL QUANTITY OF MATERIAL RECEIVED AFTER EXPEDITION
STOP WE MUST SUPPLY ALSO AERONAUTICAL STORY IN ORDER GET NECESSARY VARIETY
STOP NOBILES STORY WILL NOT BE PART OF GREAT ARTICLE SIGNED BY YOU AND
AMUNDSEN BUT INDEPENDENT SUPPLEMETARY STORY STOP UNTIL THESE ARTICLES
DELIVERED WE SHALL NOT GET LAST INSTALLMENT PRESS CONTRACTS STOP WE REGRET
THEREFORE NOT BEING ABLE COMPLY WITH YOUR WISHES AND DESIRE CALL YOUR
ATTENTION TO FACT THAT AEROCLUB ACCORDING TO CONTRACT IS SOLE ADMINISTRATIVE
AND ECONOMIC   LEADER EXPEDITION STOP WE MUST INSIST THAT THIS AGREEMENT
IS ABSURD   OTHERWISE RESULT WILL BE FAILURE TO GET ECONOMICALLIABILITIES

THOMNESSEN SVERR BRYN

Facsimile of telegram referred to on opposite page

20 WXP J. 209 VIA RCA POST

OSLO MAY 31 1926
LCD LINCOLN ELLSWORTH

NOME ALS
CONTRACT WITH NOBILE SIGNED IN PRESENCE
OF RIISER LARSEN AS REPRESENTATIVE YOU AND
AMUNDSEN HAS FOLLOWING ARTICLE QUOTE
THE FINAL ACCOUNT OF THE EXPEDITION IS TO
BE COMPILED BY AMUNDSEN ELLSWORTH AND
NOBILE IN CONNECTION WITH THOSE WHOM
THEY MAY CHOOSE AS COLLABORATORS STOP
IT IS UNDERSTOOD THAT NOBILE WILL COMPILE
THE TECHNICAL AND AERONAUTICAL PART OF
THE WORK UNQUOTE THIS IS THE ONLY EXISTING
PARAGRAPH   CONCERNING   PUBLICATION
AND SEEN IN CONNECTION WITH FACT THAT

NOBILE HAS ALREADY WRITTEN ARTICLE FOR
PUBLICATION PRESS BEFORE DEPARTURE WE
CONSIDER UNWISE AND BAD TASTE OBJECT TO
NOBILES RIGHT COLLABORATION STOP GENERAL
DISCONTENT CONTRACTING NEWS PAPERS DUE
TO SMALL QUANTITY OF MATERIAL RECEIVED
AFTER EXPEDITION STOP WE MUST SUPPLY ALSO
AERONAUTICAL STORY IN ORDER GET NECESSARY
VARIETY STOP NOBILES STORY WILL NOT BE
PART OF GREAT ARTICLE SIGNED BY YOU AND
AMUNDSEN BUT INDEPENDENT SUPPLEMENTARY
STORY STOP UNTIL THESE ARTICLES DELIVERED
WE SHALL NOT GET LAST INSTALLMENT PRESS
CONTRACTS STOP WE REGRET THEREFORE NOT
BEING ABLE COMPLY WITH YOUR WISHES AND
DESIRE CALL YOUR ATTENTION TO FACT THAT
AEROCLUB ACCORDING TO CONTRACT IS SOLE
ADMINISTRATIVE AND ECONOMIC LEADER
EXPEDITION STOP WE MUST INSIST THAT THIS
AGREEMENT IS ABSURD OTHERWISE RESULT WILL
BE FAILURE TO GET ECONOMICAL LIABILITIES
THOMMESSEN SVERR BRYN

This cablegram gave Ellsworth and me the first intimation
we had ever had that the words "and aeronautical" had
been added to a contract which Ellsworth, in March, had
demanded by cable they should not sign. Again the Aëro
Club had led us into endless difficulties by its hasty and ill-
advised action and by its lack of character in opposing the
preposterous demands of the Italian. Again Thommessen,
Sverre, and Bryn had been so eager to acquiesce in everything
that Nobile proposed, and so deferential to his most impudent
demands, that they had added this unauthorized phrase to
an unauthorized contract, and thus had provided a loophole
which, by stretching to its limits the interpretation of the

word "aeronautical," he could use as an excuse for writing almost what he pleased, and where, about any aspect of the expedition.

For a long time after the receipt of this cable, Ellsworth and I used every means of persuading Nobile to observe the plain intent of our original understanding. Failing in that, we tried to compel him to observe at the least the plain intent of even this unauthorized contract. This contract, if the words be taken in their ordinary sense and not tortured into some absurdly strange meaning, clearly intended: first, that Nobile should write nothing but one chapter for the book only; and second, that this sole chapter should be devoted exclusively to a record of his management of the dirigible as skipper. Notwithstanding this plain meaning of the terms of the contract, Nobile has written articles for the American and Italian newspapers on all aspects of the expedition, and at the time this present book is being written (in December, 1926) is engaged in an extensive lecture tour of the United States in which he is describing freely whatever he chooses about the expedition. Nobile's conduct throughout the expedition from first to last, and his conduct since, have caused me more vexation and humiliation than I can describe.

The unfamiliarity of the public with the facts I have just related has enabled Nobile to get into the minds of many people the idea that he had a major part in the conception and the execution of this epoch-making flight. The truth, on the contrary, is that his sole function in it was the function of skipper of the *Norge*. He had exactly the same relation to the success of the expedition that the captain of an American transport during the World War had to the success of the American Expeditionary Force. It is just as preposterous for Nobile to claim any other credit for this as it would be for the captain of the transport to claim that he made the American declaration of war and conceived the plans of the

SIGNAL CORPS, UNITED STATES ARMY

WASHINGTON-ALASKA MILITARY CABLE AND TELEGRAPH SYSTEM

TELEGRAM

RECEIVED at

15 WXP F 18T RADIO VIA RCA
OSLO MAY 31/1
LCD LINCOLN ELLSWORTH NOME
PART OF DOCUMENT AS FOLLOWS   QUOTE W REISEND OF NORWEGIAN
AEROCLUB GAVE REPORT THAT HE   HAD RECEIVED FROM MR ELLSWORTH
COMMUNICATION THAT ELLSWORTH WAS ONLY   TOO GLAD TO CONCEDE TO
DESIRE TO HAVE COLONEL NOBILES   NAME CONNECTED WITH EXPEDITION STOP
PRESIDENT REPORTED THAT AEROCLUB AFTER   HAVING THANKED MR ELLSWORTH WARMLY
FOR THIS PERSONAL GREAT SACRIFICE   HAD RESOLVED IN RECOGNITION OF
ITALIAN GOVERNMENT AND OF CONSTRUCTOR   OF AIRSHIP NAME EXPEDITION THE
AMUNDSEN ELLSWORTH NOBILE TRANSPOLAR   FLIGHT STOP PRESIDENT REPORTED THAT
HE WOULD MAKE THIS COMMUNICATION   ON DELIVERY OF AIRSHIP ON
29TH   OF MARCH STOP AEROCLUB   HAD ALSO RESOLVED THAT NOT
ONLY THE NORWEGIAN BUT ALSO   THE AMERICAN AND THE ITALIAN
FLAG SHOULD BE DROPPED AT   NORTHPOLE & ONLY THAT NORWEGIAN FLAG
WAS TO BE THROWN DOWN FIRST   STOP OTHERWISE THE CHANGING OF
NAME WILL EFFECT NO CHANGES   IN NATIONALITY OF EXPEDITION OR
IN THE CONTRACTS ALREADY CONCLUDED

AEROCLUB   1145

Facsimile of telegram referred to on opposite page

General Staff which led to the sending of the expedition.

To return to the chronological facts of my narrative: On the same day at Nome that Ellsworth received the cable from the Aëro Club officers, quoted above, he received also a second cable signed by the Aëro Club itself though, of course, the same men sent it. This cable reads as follows:

15 WXP F 18T RADIO VIA RCA
OSLO MAY 31/1
LCD LINCOLN ELLSWORTH NOME
PART OF DOCUMENT AS FOLLOWS QUOTE W REISEND [PRESIDENT] OF NORWEGIAN AEROCLUB GAVE REPORT THAT HE HAD RECEIVED FROM MR ELLSWORTH COMMUNICATION THAT ELLSWORTH WAS ONLY TOO GLAD TO CONCEDE TO DESIRE TO HAVE COLONEL NOBILES NAME CONNECTED WITH EXPEDITION STOP PRESIDENT REPORTED THAT AEROCLUB AFTER HAVING THANKED MR ELLSWORTH WARMLY FOR THIS PERSONAL GREAT

SACRIFICE HAD RESOLVED IN RECOGNITION OF
ITALIAN GOVERNMENT AND OF CONSTRUCTOR
OF AIRSHIP NAME EXPEDITION THE AMUNDSEN
ELLSWORTH NOBILE TRANSPOLAR FLIGHT STOP
PRESIDENT REPORTED THAT HE WOULD MAKE
THIS COMMUNICATION ON DELIVERY OF AIRSHIP
ON 29TH OF MARCH STOP AEROCLUB HAD ALSO
RESOLVED THAT NOT ONLY THE NORWEGIAN
BUT ALSO THE AMERICAN AND THE ITALIAN FLAG
SHOULD BE DROPPED AT NORTH POLE & ONLY
THAT NORWEGIAN FLAG WAS TO BE THROWN
DOWN FIRST STOP OTHERWISE THE CHANGING OF
NAME WILL EFFECT NO CHANGES IN NATIONALITY
OF EXPEDITION OR IN THE CONTRACTS ALREADY
CONCLUDED.

AEROCLUB

The only comments to be made on this cable are these:
"The communication" simply never existed. Ellsworth did
not tell anybody that he was glad to have Nobile's name
connected with the expedition. What actually happened
was that, at our second meeting in Rome, Thommessen had
urged us in piteous tones to make good what apparently he
had already promised, namely, an undertaking to permit
Nobile's name to be used in connection with the expedition
in Italy only, and even there only at the time of the taking over
of the airship from the Italian government. Thommessen
assured us in a final plea that this was intended merely as
a temporary and local compliment and as a concession to
Italian pride. Under these urgings, and for fear that, if we
did not concede that much, the Italian government would
refuse to go through with the bargain and not let us have
the ship, Ellsworth and I had reluctantly consented to that
very restricted use of Nobile's name. Later, as the cable just
quoted shows, the Aëro Club again acted like the camel in

Form 39

SIGNAL CORPS, UNITED STATES ARMY
WASHINGTON-ALASKA MILITARY CABLE AND TELEGRAPH SYSTEM
TELEGRAM

RECEIVED at

16 WXP F 84 VIA RCA POST

OSLO JUNE 4 1926

LINCOLN ELLSWORTH NOME ÁLS

HAVE ALREADY SENT THE TWO ONLY EXISTING PARAGRAPHS CONCERNING NOBILE

AND PUBLICATION STOP OWING TO AMUNDSENS WISHES EVERYTHING CONCERNING LEADER-

SHIP WAS TAKEN OUT OF AGREEMENT ROME WE CONFIRM THAT CONDITION

FOR YOUR CONTRIBUTION WAS THAT AMUNDSEN AND YOU SHOULD WRITE

BOOK BUT THIS WAS CHANGED LATER BY YOUR TELEGRAM ADMITTING

NOBILE WRITE AERONAUTICAL PART STOP CONCERNING NEWSPAPER ARTICLES NOTHING HAS

BEEN SAID BUT EVERY COURT WOULD IN THAT CASE UNDOUBTEDLY DECIDED IN

ANALOGY WITH AGREEMENT CONCERNING BOOK

THOMMESSEN SVERRE

BRYN

Facsimile of telegram referred to below

the Oriental proverb, who, when offered a finger, took the
whole hand. They took a "finger" of carefully limited assent
and made a "hand" of ridiculously generous concessions
out of it without our knowledge or agreement.

Ellsworth immediately cabled an indignant response to
these two messages and demanded further details. In reply
he received the following cable:

16 WXP F 84 VIA RCA POST
OSLO JUNE 4 1926
LINCOLN ELLSWORTH NOME ALS
HAVE ALREADY SENT THE TWO ONLY EXISTING
PARAGRAPHS CONCERNING NOBILE AND
PUBLICATION STOP OWING TO AMUNDSENS WISHES
EVERYTHING CONCERNING LEADERSHIP WAS
TAKEN OUT OF AGREEMENT ROME WE CONFIRM
THAT CONDITION FOR YOUR CONTRIBUTION WAS
THAT AMUNDSEN AND YOU SHOULD WRITE BOOK

BUT THIS WAS CHANGED LATER BY YOUR TELEGRAM
ADMITTING NOBILE WRITE AERONAUTICAL
PART STOP CONCERNING NEWSPAPER ARTICLES
NOTHING HAS BEEN SAID BUT EVERY COURT
WOULD IN THAT CASE UNDOUBTEDLY DECIDED
IN ANALOGY WITH AGREEMENT CONCERNING
BOOK

THOMMESSEN SVERRE BRYN

This cable clearly demonstrates that the officers of the Aëro Club themselves place the common-sense interpretation upon their unfortunate phrase in that unhappy and unauthorized contract. Even from their point of view, Nobile's writing of newspaper articles was wholly unauthorized.

During the five months following our arrival at Nome, and until a few weeks ago, Ellsworth and I tried by letter and cable to bring the Aëro Club of Norway to a decently repentant attitude regarding their mismanagement of our interests in the flight, and to get them to go on public record decisively in repudiation of Nobile's absurd claims. These efforts produced no satisfactory results. Perhaps it was too much to hope that they would: First, because it is human nature to dislike publicly to admit one's errors, and secondly, because Thommessen, Sverre, and Bryn had meanwhile been ceremoniously decorated with a much-coveted Italian medal and consequently would have been doubly embarrassed and deprived of an honour which they prize if they had made a candid statement of the exact facts.

In November, Ellsworth and I lost all patience with the Aëro Club's evasions of our demands for a full public statement, and in disgust we cabled our resignation from the Club. This was the, only means we had at our command to give public expression to our indignation at, their conduct.

The officers of the Aëro Club of Norway have not only avoided their plain duty to make a plain statement of the obvious facts of the controversy, but they have been guilty as well of playing up to the swelling nationalistic pride of the Italians at the expense of the honour and glory of their own country. And, finally, they have been guilty of gross ingratitude to Ellsworth. Before the *Norge* started on her flight, the Aëro Club gave Ellsworth a dinner in Oslo. At this dinner, Sverre made a speech in which he felicitated the Club upon our naming it as the official sponsor and financial agent of the flight. In this speech he declared that, "A year ago we were a puny infant, unknown outside of Norway. To-day, as a result of this expedition, we are the best known Aëro Club in the world." This declaration was loudly applauded by the other members of the Club. If the Club felt that way when the expedition was first undertaken – an expedition which was soon hailed all over the world for its triumphant success – the most elementary gratitude, as well as common frankness, should have urged them in the fall to come out with a candid statement of the facts. Ellsworth and I wanted nothing more than the facts because those facts, plainly stated, would completely vindicate our position regarding Nobile. The Aëro Club, however, appears to cherish other sentiments and has followed another course. My resignation from it was intended as a public demonstration of my disgust, and I am glad of this opportunity further to express my contempt.

To resume my narrative: Riiser-Larsen now telegraphed us, asking that we send a boat to Teller to bring him and the rest of the boys on down to Nome. I went to my old friends, the Lomen brothers, and hired one of their boats to make the trip. As I was walking down the street in Nome, on my way to see the boat, I encountered the priest of the local Catholic parish. He greeted me and, after the usual exchange of pleasantries, inquired if I was on my way "to meet Nobile." I must have looked puzzled, as naturally I was, so he showed me a telegram signed by Nobile which read: "Coming in on Coast Guard cutter."

I later got from Riiser-Larsen the details of this surprising incident, which proved to be another example of Nobile's pettiness and itch for ostentation. It seemed that Riiser-Larsen had told Nobile that I was sending the Lomen boat to bring out all the remaining members of the expedition, including the Italians. Nobile made no comment upon Riiser-Larsen's information, but it turned out later that he had immediately gone to the telegraph office and wired to the Coast Guard Service requesting that a cutter be sent to Teller for him. The Coast Guard, knowing nothing about the circumstances, had amiably obliged him. When the cutter arrived at Teller, Nobile loaded himself and his five companions on board, without any suggestion that the Norwegians be included in the party, and by this device made a separate and ostentatious entry into Nome.

The citizens of Nome maintain a residence for transient guests to whom they wish to show some special attention. This pleasant edifice is called the Log Hut. It was, I believe, originally used as a club-house, but in recent years has served the purpose just mentioned. This residence was very kindly offered to Ellsworth and myself. We found very pleasant quarters there.

For the crew we rented the best rooms in the best hotel. Nobile, however, would have none of it. He gave the impression that he felt that such small quarters were "beneath the dignity of an Italian officer" and asked that other accommodations be shown to him. He eventually settled in the largest hotel in town, which had been closed for the winter except for the quarters occupied by the host and his family. Nobile took up residence here in lonely grandeur.

Possibly Nobile had another reason, for I noticed that he was avoiding occasions to meet me, while, on the other hand, he took pains to seek out Ellsworth when I was not present. This perhaps was not un-natural , for Nobile is not an especially valorous person, and though I am by no means a savage, still Ellsworth has a good deal gentler disposition than mine, and Nobile had reason to feel that I was thoroughly irritated and aroused. Nobile confided to Ellsworth his plaintive objections to our signing our own newspaper articles, and poured into his ear further details of his "many troubles." Ellsworth finally convinced Nobile that the sensible thing to do was to come over to the Log Hut and have a full discussion among the three of us with a view to clearing up all misunderstandings.

At this conference he complained especially of two incidents. The first occurred at Teller while the *Norge* was being dissembled there. Nobile complained that the Norwegian members of the crew during that time had insisted on going off in a party by themselves to celebrate a Norwegian national holiday, May 17th. Nobile's objections to this episode were a curious mixture of wounded vanity and dignity.

The second incident had also occurred at Teller, and from Nobile's point of view was much the more serious, because it affected more deeply his most prominent characteristic, which is personal vanity. It was on a day when the motors of the *Norge* were pulled ashore. Everyone was busy helping to get these heavy objects from the ice on to the land. It was a hard job and everyone – pilot or not pilot – was supposed to lend a hand. As they were sweating and pulling, the journalist of the expedition, Ramm, suddenly discovered that Nobile stood idle with his hands in his pockets. This was more than Ramm could endure. In a burst of irritation at the sight of one inactive person in the midst of all this pressing activity, Ramm had exclaimed to Nobile: "Why don't you get to work?"

Nobile related this incident to Ellsworth and me with emotional intensity, protesting that he was an Italian officer and that such a remark was intolerably insulting. I told Nobile that his position as Italian officer had nothing to do with his position as pilot of the *Norge* and that I thought he was making much too large a matter out of Ramm's momentary outburst of temper under very trying circumstances, but that I agreed that Ramm ought not to have said what he did and that I would require Ramm to apologize if I found the conditions as he explained. However, after I had conferred with Riiser-Larsen, I dropped the matter.

Nobile now complained about our interpretation of the contract governing the expedition. He iterated and reiterated that he was "an Italian officer," and that we had not shown him the consideration to which that rank entitled him. Again I impatiently explained to him that so long as he was connected with the *Norge* expedition he was not an Italian officer, but was merely a member of the expedition. I pointed out that the expedition was not an official undertaking of any government, but was a private enterprise originated by Ellsworth and myself. Nobile had been employed to accompany it, not as an Italian officer, not as a representative of the Italian government, but as a private individual who happened, by reason of his familiarity with the dirigible, to be the most available man we could employ in the important but subordinate position of skipper of the ship.

This conference ended with Nobile still dissatisfied. Some days later, he encountered Ellsworth in the telegraph office, and a second conference was arranged at the Log Hut. Nobile opened the discussion on this occasion with a very imperious manner. He demanded full recognition as one of the three commanders of the expedition, including in these brusque demands that his name appear with Ellsworth's and mine as co-signer of the articles for the *New York Times* and of the book about the expedition. I thereupon read to him the cables addressed to Ellsworth, which have been reproduced in the preceding pages, and pointed out that they clearly limited both his status as a member of the expedition and the extent of his privilege in writing about it.

Nobile thereupon burst into a tirade which revealed fully the schemes and ambitions which had been boiling in his mind from his first connection with the expedition. This emotional oration disclosed that he had from the very beginning harboured "illusions of greatness." His vanity, feeding upon his ambition, had built up in his own mind an idea of his importance in the matter, which bore no relation either to what he had been told by us when we employed him or to the plain facts of his written contract. In his mind's eye he had seen himself throughout as a great explorer who had been seized with a vision in which he had invented the idea of a flight across the Arctic Ocean, who had then designed the ship in which the flight was to be undertaken, who had then joined forces (for reasons unexplained) with two relatively unimportant persons named Ellsworth and Amundsen, and finally had flown triumphantly across the North Pole with the eyes of the world upon him in his daring exploit. The thing that cut him to the heart evidently was that Ellsworth and I, at every stage of the proceedings, had been cruelly indifferent to this "huge cloudy vision of a high romance" that was seething in his brain, and had callously treated him at all times as an ordinary mortal, who was expected to do his job like any other member of the expedition, and to observe verbal understandings and written contracts, which, perversely enough, prevented him from turning this dream of glory into tangible reality.

Looking back over the whole series of events from the beginning, I can, of course, by exercising my imagination and sense of humour, see how Nobile got himself worked up into this state of mind, though at best I do not think the explanation is any particular tribute to his common sense or his character. The scene at Rome when we took over the *Norge* was doubtless enough to fire the fervid Latin imagination. It had been made the occasion of an outburst of Italian national feeling. Hundreds of people had crowded the field. Mussolini himself was present. Flags were flying and bands were playing. Perhaps on that day it would have been too much to expect that Nobile should not have felt that this was an official tribute to himself as an explorer, or that he should not have felt that on the expedition he represented in his person the honour and the power of the Italian nation. Even though he knew (as he did) that this was not an official but a private expedition, and even though he knew (as he did) that he was not a leader of the expedition but a paid employee, nevertheless, it would have been natural and pardonable for him, on that day, to have felt a glowing sense of his own importance. Where his folly came in was in his failure in the weeks that followed to readjust his emotions and his ideas to the sensible facts of the situation. Certainly, in Nome, by the first week of June, he should have recovered from the intoxication of that one glamorous day in sunny Italy at the end of the preceding March.

As Nobile's narration to Ellsworth and me proceeded, however, I lost all patience with his childish display of lack of common sense. When, in his peroration, he grandiloquently shouted, "I have given my life to this expedition – I had the whole responsibility of the flight," anger got the best of me. For this strutting dreamer, this epauletted Italian, who six months before had had no more thought of Arctic exploration than he had of superseding Mussolini as the Chief of State, to be shouting this kind of presumptuous nonsense in my face, with my thirty years of labour and achievement in the Polar regions, and to be claiming an equal share with us in the conception and execution of the transarctic flight, with his silly talk about giving his life to the expedition and having the whole responsibility of it

– all this was too much for me to stomach. With furious indignation, I reminded him now in no uncertain tones of the pitiable spectacle he would have presented on the Polar ice if the *Norge* had by chance been forced down, and pointed out how preposterous would have been his claims to effective leadership under those conditions. And in heated tones that carried finality I reminded him, for the last time, that Ellsworth and I were the leaders of the expedition, that we should never recognize his right to claim a major share in its achievement, and that we would prevent him, if we could, from writing anything about it except what his contract permitted him to write about the technical aspects of the flight.

Nobile took this stinging rebuke with becoming meekness. The swaggering officer who had entered the door a little earlier left it with a return to his more natural childish manner. His only response as he left was a hopeless shrug of the shoulders and a mumbled remark that he was "sick of the whole thing." And well he might be – the breaking of the bubble of one's own pretensions, however salutary, is never pleasant.

If Nobile got no balm for his wounded feelings from Ellsworth and me, who knew the facts about his pretensions, he did get it from the citizens of Nome, who did not know. So effectively did he spread the story of his Polar achievement – a task in which he had the indefatigable assistance of the local priest above mentioned – that when people in Nome gave a public banquet celebrating the *Norge* flight, Nobile was the guest of the evening and Ellsworth and I were not invited. I except from all criticisms of Nome a few of my friends of many years' standing, including the Lomen brothers, who are generally accepted as the leading citizens of Alaska, having done most of all its inhabitants for the permanent development of the territory, and being the leaders in the business life of Nome and the surrounding region. Their loyal friendship has followed me without wavering through all the years of our acquaintanceship, and I am their debtor many times over for kindnesses both personal and financial. The general run of the people in Nome, however, acted like the masses everywhere – they were credulous of marvellous tales, easily moved to emotion, and eager to make a one-day sensation over the latest novelty in the way of popular heroes. Ellsworth and I were an old story – we had been there before – whereas Nobile was a novelty. He had, besides, the glamour of the Roman ovation about him. Naturally, I keenly felt the slight put upon Ellsworth, my comrades, and myself by this public demonstration which ignored us. It was the climax of a series of incidents of the same tenor, and I should be less than candid if I did not record it and express my feeling that the whole situation revealed bad taste and bad manners on the part of the people of Nome.

On a beautiful day in June, all the members of the expedition left Nome on the steamship *Victoria* for Seattle. Amid the numerous irritations of that period, it is pleasant to recall that, on the voyage, Nobile's five Italian subordinates, in private conversation with some of our Norwegians, expressed their cordial disapproval of Nobile's conduct since the expedition landed. A phrase spoken by one of them was greeted with approval by the others and deserves quotation: "We sympathize with you in this matter, but what can we do?"

As the vessel approached Seattle, Ellsworth and I rallied each other upon the appearance we should present before the crowd which we understood was to meet us at the dock. We had brought no money with us from Spitzbergen, and in keeping with Nobile's constant injunctions about the minimum weight of luggage, we had brought no change of clothing with us. Consequently, in Nome, when we discarded our Arctic costumes, we had bought and donned the only clothes available, and these were the apparel of the miner. Our rough suits, woollen shirts, and heavy shoes were appropriate enough on the streets of Nome in midwinter, but, however picturesque, they were hardly fitted to the formalities of an official civic reception in Seattle. Nevertheless, there was nothing to be done about it. We had the consolation of feeling that, at any rate, all the members of our party were in the same situation.

Imagine, then, our astonishment when, as the vessel drew up toward the pier, Nobile appeared from below apparelled in the most resplendent dress uniform of a colonel in the Italian army. This was nothing less than double dealing. By constant admonitions on the subject of little baggage, which the rest of us had accepted in good faith, he had prevented us from bringing even decently presentable clothing on the expedition across the Pole; and again, on the flight from Rome to Oslo, had caused actual physical suffering to the Norwegians who had been required to make the trip insufficiently clad. Nobile's selfish violation of his own admonitions in the matter of the flags put overboard at the North Pole had only caused us a slight amused irritation; but now it was revealed that he had secreted in the *Norge* on the flight across the Arctic Ocean – where, according to his own story, every needless pound was a menace to the very lives of us all – the bulk and weight of heavy military uniforms, not only for himself, but for two of his compatriots!

These thoughts, added to our irritation at his vulgar bad taste in appearing on this occasion in ostentatious contrast of appearance with his fellow members of the expedition, caused me to boil inwardly. My anger was increased when it became apparent that he had carefully calculated the spot at which the gangplank would be let down from the deck, and had stationed himself at a point beside it where he could thrust himself forward and seem to lead the expedition off the vessel. Notwithstanding my indignation and contempt, I made no effort to thwart him. Certainly, it was beneath my dignity to enter a competition for the moment's precedence with this strutting upstart.

An officer of the *Victoria,* however, also sensed this intended impudence of Nobile's, and, with the true seaman's punctiliousness regarding the proprieties, quietly but very firmly placed himself in a position to block Nobile's dash for the gangplank, and then bowed to me and Ellsworth to lead the procession to the landing.

There a large crowd was gathered to receive us, including official representatives of the city government. A charming little girl, six or eight years of age, dressed in a gay frock, stepped forward with a bouquet of flowers, in a pretty little ceremony of greeting. Here, in miniature, Nobile had the triumph for which his uniform was a part of the planning. The little girl did the most natural thing in the world: Seeing before her three strange men, and realizing only that the occasion was the most important in her young life, and seeing also that two of the men were roughly dressed like workmen, while the third was resplendent in a military uniform, there could be but one answer in her mind to the question of relative importance. Naturally, the military uniform got the flowers!

In Seattle, too, Italian propaganda had created a situation which caused me sharp disappointment. The Italian Consul had evidently received instructions from the Italian government to do everything possible to make Nobile's return a triumph. In this task, his efforts were ably seconded by the local Italian Fascisti. By their volubility and patriotic fervour, they had succeeded in creating the impression in Seattle, before our arrival, that the *Norge* flight was largely an Italian undertaking, and that Nobile was, with us, the chief in command of it. This idea got so firmly fixed in the minds of the local committee that, at the first luncheon tendered us, though I was given the first place of honour,

Nobile was seated in the next place and Ellsworth in the third.

Ellsworth was far too much the gentleman to mention to anyone but myself (his confidential and intimate friend) the hurt to his pride involved in this mistaken arrangement. After the luncheon, however, I felt it to be my duty to call upon the responsible members of the Official Committee of Welcome and point out to them that, by every right, Ellsworth was entitled to share absolutely on an equality with me in whatever honours the expedition had earned; whereas Nobile belonged in a distinctly lower category. As a result, the mistake was corrected at later gatherings.

My misadventures with the Aëro Club of Norway broke out anew in the summer of 1926, after our safe arrival in Alaska with the *Norge*. Upon our return to the United States, the Aëro Club publicly accused me of postponing the sending of the news of our success to the *New York Times* so long as nearly to make the *Times* break its contract for its publication. This was a silly charge to make, because we had taken on the *Norge* an experienced newspaper correspondent for the express purpose of having him handle this matter in an expeditious and professional manner. I had foreseen that I would be intensely busy on our arrival and had taken this newspaper man along purposely that he might take this burden off my shoulders. His only function was to prepare this material at the earliest possible moment, submit it to me for my corrections and O. K., and transmit it at once to the *Times*. The newspaper man had properly remained at Teller to record the last happenings at the dissembling of the *Norge,* whilst Ellsworth and I had gone on down to Nome. He did his work faithfully, but owing to the difficulties with the radio at Teller, the news leaked out from Nome and the fact of our arrival became public property. It must also be known that Nobile sent out full reports of the voyage to Italy which were widely published all over the world and nearly caused a break with the New York *Times*.

One of the worst features of the Aëro Club's mismanagement was its handling of the motion pictures. When Ellsworth and I returned to Spitzbergen in the *N-25*, in the summer of 1925, after being lost on the Arctic ice for more than three weeks, our sudden and dramatic reappearance, when we were supposed to be dead, created a news interest all over the world. Mr Bruce Johnson, of the First National Pictures, offered to the Aëro Club for $50,000 the motion pictures of our flight and return. The Aëro Club fatuously refused the offer, declaring that they could do better. To the best of my knowledge, this stupid error cost us $42,000. These efforts were silly on their face, for anybody with the slightest knowledge of the motion-picture business realizes that the great market is the United States, and that the value of news pictures diminishes in geometrical ratio with the passage of time between the events they portray and the day they are exhibited in the theatres.

Even if the Aëro Club had not realized these facts in 1925, their experience of that year should have taught them something by which to profit in 1926. They were handling all the business matters of the *Norge* flight, and the motion-picture operator on the expedition acted under their orders. The immediate development of these films and their prompt sale in the United States should have been the first thought of the Club. I have no doubt that they could have been sold at once to an American producer for $75,000. But what did the Aëro Club do? Incredible as it may seem, they made no effort to dispose of the pictures at once in America, but actually transported them clear to Oslo, and had them developed there.

Meanwhile, I was getting utterly disgusted with the Club's mismanagement. In September, 1926, I demanded that Bryn, the man whom I held chiefly responsible for it, be ousted from any connection with our business affairs. The Club replied that they could not even consider my demand, and thereupon I informed them that I could not work with them any more, and that, for the protection of my own interests, I would thenceforth look out for my business concerns myself.

Realizing that the Club was about to repeat its blunder of 1925 with the films of 1926, I went to the photographer, who had the original film in his possession, and directed him to make me two complete copies and give them to me. When I had them in my possession, I notified the Aëro Club that I would give them fourteen days in which to get an offer for the films, failing which I proposed to get such value as I could out of them for myself by using them in connection with my lectures.

My ultimatum was greeted with jeers. "What," they exclaimed, "can you do about the movies? You have not got any of the films." "Oh, yes, I have," I retorted. "I have been too long in this business to be fooled by greenhorns like you." I then told them that I had two copies of the films safely in my possession and that, if they did not meet my demands by getting an offer within the two weeks, I should then consider myself morally free to get such value out of them as I could for myself.

Later, the Aëro Club made a nasty public statement which they issued and in which they came as near as they dared to calling me a thief by indirect language. Indeed, their language was not translatable into English otherwise than by the ugly word "theft," and it was so translated and published broadcast in dispatches to American newspapers. I have no idea how many people read this libel, but doubtless thousands did and have got the idea in their minds that I had actually stolen from the Aëro Club something that really belonged to them. The fact of the matter, of course, is that I merely took out of their hands the control of my own property which, as my agents, they had grossly mismanaged. Even in doing this, I assured them that I would use only 500 metres of the 1,500 metres of the film. This one third of the pictures I would not sell, but would use only to illustrate my lectures, which would indeed be a very good advertisement for the rest of the film.

How seriously the Club itself really regarded its own charge of theft will appear from a letter I received from Oslo, dated December 20, 1926, and written by J. Chr. Gundersen, the, Norwegian film magnate, to whom the Club in turn had handed over the film for sale. Mr Gundersen wrote in Norwegian. The following is a translation of the substance of this letter:

"I repeat the permission to use 500 metres (one third) of the film... Will you not be good enough to announce from the stage that this is only part of the big Polar film soon to be shown in America."

Gundersen's letter goes on to request me to go to the film companies in the United States and see what I can do about interesting them in it – something which should have been done, of course, six months earlier (in July) by the Aëro Club itself when it first had the film complete and when there was an eager market for it.

When all the expenses of the *Norge* flight had been accounted for, it appeared that the expedition was still about $75,000 in debt. Not all of it is a legal obligation. Nowhere near all of it is a moral obligation. I have done and shall continue to do everything in my power to repay all of it that I regard as a moral obligation. My lecture tour of the spring of 1927 is being devoted to that purpose, as is also a second lecture tour already contracted for in 1928. Likewise , all the royalties on the book I wrote about the *Norge* expedition recently published in Norway are being applied to this end. To what extent I shall pay any attention to obligations nominally resting upon me toward the Aëro Club remains to be seen. If its management had been competent, there would have been no deficit at all.

A final example of the Club's mismanagement: When I arrived in the United States on November 27, 1926, I was met at the dock by my lecture manager, Mr Lee Keedick, with the incredible news that Nobile was already touring the United States delivering a lecture on the *Norge* flight! When I recovered from my astonishment, I instantly cabled to Norway to find out if the Aëro Club had consented to this clear breach of Nobile's bargain, and pointed out that this Italian was travelling all over the country telling false things about the expedition and dragging the name of Norway in the dirt. To my even greater amazement, the Aëro Club replied that this tour was being made with their permission. Here was Nobile lecturing in America for his own profit, covering the field ahead of me, while I was to follow him lecturing solely to pay the debt due to other follies of mismanagement on the part of the Aëro Club. Morally, I feel that this situation relieves me of all obligations to pay the debt – nevertheless, I do intend to pay it. All the creditors will be paid as my means permit, in the measure of the justice of their claims.

In Nobile's lectures in the United States he has repeatedly declared that Mussolini originated the idea of the *Norge* Polar flight. He has been charged in the public press with making other misstatements about the flight, and he has written to the papers specifically denying some of these charges, but he has never denied this one. There is plenty of proof that he has made this preposterous claim for Mussolini. In the interest of truth it is, therefore, fortunate that a book has recently been published in Oslo under the title *The Norge Expedition: Behind the Scenes*. The author is Odd Arnesen, of the staff of the *Aftenposten* of Oslo. In this book, Arnesen records that his chief, Frois Froisland, the editor in chief of the *Aftenposten,* had an interview with Mussolini in Rome immediately after the news reached the world of the successful conclusion of the *Norge* flight. Among other things in this interview, Mussolini said to Froisland:

Please, convey my warmest congratulations to the countrymen of Roald Amundsen. In this moment of victory, we must not forget that Amundsen is the creator of the expedition. It was he who launched the idea of exploring the Polar regions from the air.

I should like at this point to introduce a final bit of evidence regarding the *Norge* matter. Not least among the pleasant distinctions that have fallen to me do I count my membership in what is probably the most exclusive club in the world. This is the Polar Legion, originated on December 17, 1926, by Mr Lincoln Ellsworth, Commander Richard E. Byrd, and myself. We included in the charter membership, though dead, the only other two men in history who could qualify under the terms of membership "which demands leadership of an expedition which has reached either the geographic North or South Pole." The Club is not likely ever to be crowded – though possibly Magellan may have thought the same thing about the Circumnavigators' Club, which now has a numerous membership. Aside from everything else, however, the organization of the Club, with its present membership, gratifyingly indicates that Commander Byrd shares with Ellsworth and me our opinion of Nobile's claims to leadership in the *Norge* expedition.

This concludes my faithful narration of the truth of the *Norge* flight. To write it has been a painful task – foreign alike to my inclination and to my usual practice. It would have been much pleasanter to me to have let the unfortunate episodes of that expedition rest in the oblivion of things well forgotten. There they would have rested, were it not that this is my autobiography and that, for the sake of my record as an explorer, and for the sake of my comrades on this trip, I dare not leave to chance the correction of the gross misrepresentations and impudent assumptions of Commander Nobile. Truth in the abstract, as well as justice to my own reputation, demanded the foregoing record of the facts.

Perhaps it is necessary that I should add one further commentary, lest the reader, unfamiliar with the details of my life, may draw the inference that I am by nature of a jealous disposition. I am sure no one who knows me personally would ever accuse me of that. But to the public it may be worth while to demonstrate it. When I discovered the South Pole, I took with me all the members of our expedition who could possibly be provisioned for that final dash and who were equipped physically and by experience to share its toils and hazards. Fifteen years later, when, through the generosity of Mr Ellsworth, the opportunity was offered me to realize another dream of my life, to fly across the Arctic Ocean from Europe to North America by way of the North Pole, it gave me the greatest satisfaction to be able to invite to go with me one of those four gallant Norwegians who had stood with me on the South Pole. Oscar Wisting was that man. If I had been jealous of other people's honours, if I had been ungenerous, I should to-day enjoy the undisputed distinction of being the only man in the world who had been at both the Poles. To me, however, that distinction would bring far less pleasure than does the thought that I have been able to make it possible for that gallant companion, that loyal friend, that brave comrade, Wisting, to share with me always the honour of being the first to visit both Poles.

And, I may add, to share with me the honours of the last great undertaking of my life. For I am here confiding to the reader that I consider my career as an explorer closed. It has been granted to me to achieve what I set out to do. That is honour enough for one man. Henceforward, I shall always take a lively interest in the yet unsolved scientific phenomena of the distant Polar Regions, but I cannot hope to find a possible field of achievement as important as that which lies behind me. I shall, therefore, rest content with these scientific problems and shall devote the most of my time to writing and lecturing, and to the pleasures of associations with my many friends in America and Europe.

These friends, after all, are perhaps the source of the fullest possible enjoyment in life. My explorations have brought me welcome formal honours, but, better than these, they have brought me the joys of enduring friendships. Many of my best friends are Americans. Their homes are open to me and their hearts as well. I enter both with deep thanksgiving and an enduring satisfaction.

CHAPTER IX

Concerning
Mr Stefansson And Others

A dmiral Peary was the first man ever to reach the North
Pole.

"But," you may ask, "how do you know he reached it?
You have only his word for it. He went there practically
alone – of course, the Negro Hanson was too ignorant to
know whether they reached it or not. And of course, too,
Peary, with his technical knowledge, could easily have faked
his records."

Nevertheless, I know Admiral Peary reached the North
Pole. The reason I know it is that I knew Peary. What you
say about his ability to fake his observations is perfectly
true. The answer to any doubt on that score is simply that
Peary was not that kind of man.

The character of the explorer, therefore, is always the
best evidence of the truth of his claims of achievement. It
so happens that my claim to the capture of the South Pole
rests not only on my word but also on the testimony of my
unfortunate competitor, the gallant Captain Scott, whose
diary records his finding our tent and notes when he reached
the Pole three weeks later. But, after all, even this testimony
– tragically preserved, from the dead hand of a competitor
in the race – is really of less value, as evidence, than the
evidence of my personal character as it has been written by
my whole life. Both Scott and I might have made mistakes

in our observations. Indeed, when the scientists got through checking over my observations, after my return from the South Pole, they found an error in every one of them, but it was a "constant" error, in the mathematical sense, and it proved, not that the observations were unskillfully made, but that there exists in the Polar region an undetermined natural phenomenon that affects solar observations. This very constant error was, in the minds of the scientists, the strongest proof that my observations were made in good faith. If I had been trying to fake data, I should have had to be a very clever mathematician to dream of faking them that way.

Like all explorers who understand their business, I realized at the South Pole the possibility of error in observations and in calculations of position. As I wished to have the satisfaction, forever after, of feeling sure that I had stood on the exact site of the South Pole, I and my companions spent three days in exploring an area, ten miles in radius, around the spot our calculations showed us was presumably the Pole. Thus we made sure that we had compensated for any possible error.

The foregoing paragraphs have been written chiefly to illuminate the only comment I feel called upon to make on the Cook-Peary controversy: Polar records *must be read in the light of the antecedents of the explorers.*

My experience leads me to believe that the two famous "discoveries" of Vilhjalmur Stefansson should be taken with many grains of salt. I refer respectively to Stefansson's widely heralded "Blond Eskimos" and to his equally famous "Friendly Arctic."

To deal with the "Blond Eskimos" first. It is, of course, not beyond the bounds of possibility that some small tribe of Eskimos might have escaped the observation of white men heretofore, but to say that this is likely is to stretch the possibilities much too far. Such statements should be supported by positive proof and I have heard of no such proof.

The probable explanation of the "Blond Eskimos" is perfectly obvious. The Arctic regions have been a favourite field of explorers for four hundred years. Expedition after expedition of white men has gone into that region, and most of them have wintered there. In addition to these explorers, unnumbered fur traders have pressed northward, generation after generation. In all these enterprises, the British and the Scandinavians have by far outnumbered all other races. The squawman is an invariable phenomenon of all frontiers, to say nothing of those inevitable promiscuous relations that have dotted the American West with half-breeds, the South with mulattos, and Latin-America with mestizos. The Eskimos have no higher moral code than any other people – witness the offer made to a member of the crew of the *Maud by* an Eskimo husband who volunteered to exchange the favours of his wife for one heavy steel needle.

Blond Eskimos are almost certainly half-breed grandchildren of half-breed Eskimo mothers and fair-haired, blue-eyed white fathers from the Northern countries. Anyone with even a rudimentary knowledge of the Mendelian Law governing the inheritance of physical characteristics knows perfectly well that, in the second generation of hybrids (whether plants, animals, or men), the offspring at times will revert completely to the type of one of the ancestors alone, to the exclusion of all of the characteristics of the other. The origin of Stefansson's "Blond Eskimos" in the North, therefore, can be explained, I believe, by the natural intermingling of races as often happens in like circumstances.

Stefansson's " Blond Eskimos," it seems to me, is simply a far-fetched idea. His "Friendly Arctic," however, is likely to give dangerous ideas to inexperienced explorers. No gullible person will come to any harm by believing that some Eskimos are blond. But it is entirely possible that some adventurous spirits, seeking a fresh thrill in the North, may be misled by this talk about the "friendliness" of the Arctic and will actually attempt to take advantage of this "friendliness," and venture into those regions equipped only with a gun and some ammunition. If they do, certain death awaits them: In my opinion, based on long experience and careful study, even a good marksman cannot "live off the country" in the Arctic. It is conceivable, I suppose, that a very skillful and experienced explorer, in extraordinarily favourable circumstances, with weather and game conditions just right, and close to solid land, might for a very short time "live off the country," but I would not try it myself. I would consider it sheer suicide. I do not believe it can be done.

There is just enough colourful truth in what Stefansson says to make his statement sound plausible. There is some game on the mainland and on some of the larger islands within the Arctic Circle. If one is very expert in finding it, and very skillful in capturing it, and if the luck of the season is good, he may live precariously along the fringes of the land, though it should be pointed out that starvation is a not un-common thing even with the Eskimos, who have every advantage of experience and incentive to excel in this field.

But go out on the great ice field of the Arctic, out of sight of land, and any man's chances of "living off the country" are just about equal to his chances of finding a gold mine on the top of an iceberg. There are, to be sure, a few – a very few – seals that at times come up through the ice, but seeing a seal and killing it are two very different matters. Fishing is out of the question with ice from three feet to twelve feet in thickness.

It is difficult for men living in comfort in civilized countries to realize the harshness of the Arctic, so the "Friendly Arctic" has given to many an entirely wrong impression of the care, experience, equipment, and planning necessary to merely stay alive in the far North. I have had men express astonishment at the elaborate preparations made by me to carry abundant food in concentrated form for use on my expeditions. They have been even led to believe that a march to the North Pole is little more than a light-hearted hunting expedition, upon which one leisurely advances across the ice, stopping occasionally to kill something to eat and wandering on his way with no cares about to-morrow's food.

I would not be so critical of Stefansson's tales of the "Friendly Arctic" were it not that such talk about the North is a positive injury to the whole cause of exploration. Poor judgment is sometimes understandable, if not readily forgiven; and many people have been forgiven for it, but statements that mislead and endanger the unsophisticated are unpardonable.

More than one Arctic leader has had dissensions in his expedition. Other expeditions have failed. An account of causes of failure is useful if it serves as a warning against the making of like mistakes in like circumstances. Too optimistic statements, on the contrary, are dangerous.

The most extreme example of the unfit explorer whom I have ever encountered, crossed my path in Spitzbergen in 1901. He was a captain lieutenant in the German navy, named Bauendahl. When I ran across him, he had just completed a perfectly insane attempt for the North Pole, and was just starting on an equally insane expedition for the same objective but with a new method. His scheme of the year before was to build an overhead railroad track from Spitzbergen to the Pole. This idea of his was a perfect illustration of the common human failing of inventing a plausible solution of a problem by considering only one of its obvious aspects. Bauendahl had perceived what all previous Arctic explorers had experienced, namely, that a prime difficulty in reaching the North Pole lay in the extraordinarily rough surface of the ice in the Polar Sea. This ice surface is broken into myriads of irregular hummocks, ranging in bulk from the size of a brick to the size of a house. Bauendahl's reasoning must have been something like this: "The rough surface of the ice makes it difficult to transport the supplies necessary to sustain life on the march to the Pole. Therefore I will build a railway with an overhead track, so that the rough surface of the ice will make no difference."

The silly fellow actually wasted a lot of time and money trying to put this scheme into practice. He brought from Germany to Spitzbergen a large number of heavy poles, to be set up in the ice at intervals, and heavy wire to stretch between them. Some kind of a car was to hang by an overhead wheel which should roll on this wire as a track. Bauendahl got a few miles of this absurd tramway built before the patience of his workmen gave out.

Of course, Bauendahl was crazy. If his earlier tramway did not demonstrate his insanity, certainly his next foolish scheme, which he had in progress when I met him in 1901, would convict him in the mind of any experienced worker in the North. He had got together a lot of logs from Andree's balloon house at Spitzbergen, and had bound them together to form a raft. A tug was to tow this raft to the edge of the pack ice, whence he intended to row through the ice to the east coast of Greenland, and from there he would try to obtain a higher latitude than any of his predecessors. His idea, of course, was that such a raft would resist the crushing impact of the floating ice, and would offer a broad, secure base on which to erect comfortable quarters, in which he would row to Greenland, much as Tom Sawyer and Huckleberry Finn drifted down the Mississippi River.

The old-timers in Spitzbergen were at first only amused at this wild proposal. When they discovered that the man was in earnest about it, they asked me, as an act of common humanity, to go and present to him our combined solemn protest, based upon our experience with the Arctic ice. I executed this mission with all the tact I could summon, but was received as most volunteer advisers are. I made not the slightest impression upon Bauendahl.

His sole companion on this crazy enterprise was to be a Norwegian boy. I resolved, at any cost, to save this boy's life, so I went to him and earnestly pointed out the folly of the undertaking. The boy was entirely noncommittal in his response to my urgings, but I could see from a twinkle in his eye that he was nobody's fool and had no more idea than I of risking his life on such a venture. I concluded that he felt perfectly satisfied to draw his wages for the work of preparation, but that, when the raft should actually be cut adrift in Greenland, he would not be among its passengers.

The boy did even better than I had guessed. He put out from Spitzbergen with Bauendahl on the tug, with the raft in tow behind. The night before the expedition reached the pack ice, the boy slipped out in the dark to the stern of the tug, and cut the raft adrift. When morning came and all hands appeared on deck, the raft was nowhere to be seen, and Bauendahl's expedition came to an inglorious end. Captious moralists may complain that the Norwegian boy's conduct was essentially wrong. On the other hand, he certainly saved Bauendahl's life. I leave the verdict to the reader.

Insanity among would-be explorers is rare, but almost equivalent foolhardiness is less uncommon. The first attempt at Arctic exploration in the air was made by Andree, the Swedish balloonist. A sensation of the world for two seasons, and a tragedy at its end, this attempt was never taken seriously by real explorers, who understood the practical madness of the undertaking. Andree had, before this, made a number of highly successful long-distance flights in a free balloon. These flights were dangerous, but they did not amount to practical suicide. Risky as it may be to go up in the basket of a round balloon, and drift for days wherever the chance of the winds may take you, at least – if the venture is made over a continent – there is a reasonable hope of escape in an emergency. But to undertake to drift across 1,800 miles of Arctic Ocean, with only the luck of the winds for rudder, is exactly the sort of risk the serious explorer does not take. Andree left Spitzbergen and to this day no trace of him or his balloon has ever been discovered. Doubtless, the poor fellow was forced to the ice in the Polar regions, and long ere this his balloon and his body have been engulfed in the Arctic Sea. But let us take off our hats to the brave man.

CHAPTER X

The Serious Business
Of Exploration

I Find that most people think of "adventure" when the word "exploration" is used. It may, therefore, be well to explain in detail the difference between the two words from the explorer's point of view. I do not mean to belittle the thirst for adventure. It is a perfectly natural longing for excitement that affects any man in normal health. Doubtless, it is an inheritance of our race from those remote ancestors whose struggle for existence involved the uncertainties of the chase, the hazards of combat with wild beasts, and the perils of the unknown. To them, life was a constant adventure, and the thrill that suffuses us in reproducing their experience is the normal thrill of healthy nerves reacting to the natural struggle for self-preservation. Our ancestors had to take the chances of death to get their daily livelihood. When we "flirt with death," we are going back to the compensating nervous pleasure of primitive man, which protected and elevated him in his daily struggle.

To the explorer, however, adventure is merely an unwelcome interruption of his serious labours. He is looking, not for thrills, but for facts about the unknown. Often his search is a race with time against starvation. To him, an adventure is merely a bit of bad planning, brought to light by the test of trial. Or it is unfortunate exemplification of the fact that no man can grasp all the possibilities of the future. Every explorer has adventures. He gets a thrill out of them, and he takes pleasure in thinking back upon them. But he never goes about looking for them. Exploration is too serious a business.

Not all would-be explorers realize this truth. The result is many a grave needlessly occupied before its time, and many a blasted hope.

Serious work in exploration calls for as definite and as rigorous professional preparation as does success in any other serious work in life. Infinite harm has been done to the true profession of exploring by the entrance into the field of all sorts of people who have had no proper place in it. Some of these people are mere adventurers looking for another thrill. Some are notoriety seekers looking for a quick road to an empty fame. At least one whom I have known was crazy. Many of these men have lost their lives to no useful purpose whatsoever. This is bad enough, but the worst of it is that they have cast such a doubt in the minds of sober people upon the whole field of exploration that most of the world thinks of all exploration as mere foolhardiness. This state of mind has made it extremely difficult for serious explorers like Nansen, Peary, and others to obtain funds for their work, or even to secure an opportunity to explain their serious scientific intentions in undertaking it. Few people, except a few scientists who specialize in meteorology, oceanography, geography, etc., have the slightest idea of what explorers are accomplishing, or have the slightest ability to distinguish between serious workers in exploration and the host of adventurous publicity seekers and charlatans.

The first qualification of an explorer is a sound and trained body. Exploring involves the hardest kind of physical exertion, and the capacity to endure such exertion under stress both for long periods of sustained endeavour and in the trying moments of emergency. How preposterous, then, it is for men who have lived at desks to maturity suddenly to attempt these arduous enterprises! How absurd also for men whose whole experience of life has been among the conveniences of civilization suddenly to undertake a mode of life in which everything is primitive, and for which the training of the fur trader or the whaling seaman is of infinitely more value than a college education. A great part of my success in Arctic work came from my carefully trained physique and from my hard-won apprenticeship to the actual life of the wilderness.

After the physical equipment essential to an explorer comes his mental equipment. I do not mean only the natural endowment of brains. With the exception of the one crazy man I have mentioned, all the men I have known who have led expeditions of any sort in the Arctic regions have been men of good intelligence, and some of them have been men of very high education. What I have in mind, rather, is the specialized mental equipment, which is informed regarding the experience of all preceding expeditions. This knowledge in my own case has several times saved me from serious mistakes. For example, the reader may recall that my choice of a base in the Antarctic on the Bay of Whales, which so largely contributed to our success in reaching the South Pole, was made as a result of a careful comparison of every existing description of that part of the Antarctic glacier, from its discovery by Sir John Ross in 1842 down to the year before we started South. Second-hand experience out of books is often as good as first-hand, if the reader has had enough practical experience in the same field to understand and apply what he reads.

The explorer's mental equipment – I mean if he intends to do serious work that justifies the hazards of his undertaking – must also include a thorough understanding of the scientific problems in the solution of which his explorations can have an essential part. And, finally, the explorer must understand perfectly the use of scientific instruments with which he may make observations of sufficient accuracy to be useful to the scientists to whom he brings them home.

The foregoing sketch of the qualifications of a serious explorer will, I hope, convince the reader that exploring is a highly technical and serious profession, calling for laborious years of physical and mental preparation, and having for its objective matters of importance far beyond the mere thrills of the adventurer and the cheap, brief fame of charlatans and notoriety seekers.

Arctic exploration of a serious character dates far back in history. As I have explained earlier in this book, the British for four centuries had sent expeditions to attempt the Northwest Passage. These expeditions were carefully planned, and they were outfitted and managed according to the best knowledge of their times. Though they invariably resulted in failure, and frequently in disaster, they did not fail for lack of care in planning. And they achieved scientific information of great value.

The search for the North Pole was likewise undertaken by many serious-minded men. They, too, made a good deal of progress. But the best that could be done by their methods was Lockwood's achievement of reaching his farthest north.

Dr Fridtjof Nansen revolutionized Polar exploration. He worked out new methods, based upon profound reasoning about the nature of the problem. He invented practical means to apply these measures. The result was his sensational advance over Lockwood's record, to 86° 14' N., or about 200 nautical miles nearer the Pole than any man before him had ever been.

The story of Dr Nansen and the *Fram*, as described in his *Farthest North*, is familiar to practically everybody. Unless, however, one has read and pondered the technical details underlying the events described in that thrilling narrative, he

194

cannot realize that Dr Nansen's achievement in the technical methods of Arctic exploration was vastly more important even than his sensational distance record, or than the actual scientific observations made on the *Fram* expedition.

Dr Nansen's epochal achievement in Polar work was his invention of a new method. He it was who first realized the value of dogs and light sleds as means of transport in the North. He first threw aside the heavy sledges that had broken the backs and the hearts of all previous explorers, substituting for them scientifically designed sledges of greater strength and infinitely less weight. By this invention, he easily doubled the travelling radius of men and dogs. The *Fram* expedition was a brilliant demonstration of the correctness of his theory and of the practical utility of his invention. Without his work, our capture of the South Pole would equally have been impossible. I realized the revolutionary importance of Nansen's method; I adapted it to my purposes; and I succeeded with it. No just appraisal of successful Polar exploration can be made that leaves out of reckoning the fundamental importance of Dr Nansen's work. He was the pioneer, both in theory and in practice, who made success possible.

Strangely enough, Dr Nansen has lived to see his method become obsolete. To-day, the dog and the sledge have wholly outlived their usefulness in the Arctic as instruments of exploration. Their place now, though forever glorious, is in the museum and the history books.

Aircraft has supplanted the dog. The Wright brothers and Count Zeppelin are the pioneers of the new method. The future of Polar exploration lies in the air. I make bold to claim for myself the distinction of being the first serious Polar explorer to realize this fact, and the first to give a practical demonstration of its future possibilities. I prepared, in 1909, to undertake geographical reconnaissance of Polar regions from the air, and went so far as to employ a pilot for this purpose. In 1914, I bought a Farnam 'plane and learned to fly it myself. In 1921-22, I made several attempts to undertake this work again, this time from Point Barrow. It was not, however, until 1925 that sufficient funds and the right 'planes became available, through the generosity of Mr Lincoln Ellsworth, and we made our first flight from Spitzbergen. Though that expedition did not take us, as we had hoped, from continent to continent across the Pole, it did, nevertheless, indicate both the certainty that such a flight was only a matter of time and improved devices, and that geographical observations made from the air would be of the highest value.

In 1926, with Mr Ellsworth, I commanded the expedition which made the first continent-to-continent flight across the North Pole. This flight was successful in every sense of the word, and proved, beyond further doubt, by practical demonstration, the permanent utility of aircraft in Polar exploration.

"What is the good of Arctic exploration?"

How many times that question has been put to me! Doubtless, every serious explorer has had it put to him numberless times.

The most practical value of Polar exploration is the new knowledge it provides to science regarding the phenomena of terrestrial magnetism and regarding the nature of the climate and winds in those regions (which are the weather makers of the world). Elsewhere in this book I have elaborated somewhat on both these points, but here I would add that the greatest advance likely soon to be made in the accurate prediction of day-to-day weather in the North Temperate Zone will come from the erection and maintenance of permanent weather observatories on the north coasts of America, Europe, and Asia. These observatories, completely encircling the Polar Sea, and reporting several times daily by wireless to some central station, will provide far more reliable and valuable information upon which to base weather predictions than has heretofore ever been made available to man. I got some conception of how important such a chain of observatories could be by the excited gratitude of scientists that was aroused when twice daily wireless reports of the weather encountered by the *Maud* off the north coast of Asia were sent.

The other "good" of Polar exploration cannot be so definitely translated into terms of human comfort or of money saved to the world. Personally, however, I have no doubt that it is of equal value. Whatever remains to man unknown, in this world of ours, is by so much a burden on the spirits of all men. It remains a something that man has not yet conquered – a continuing evidence of his weakness, an unmet challenge to his mastery over nature. By the same token, every mystery made plain, every unknown land explored, exalts the spirit of the whole human race – strengthens its courage and exalts its spirit permanently. The trail breaker is an indispensable ally of the spiritual values which advance and sustain civilization.

CHAPTER XI

Problems Of Food
And Equipment

I Shall devote this chapter to a description of certain aspects of our dash to the South Pole, describing here only such things as will illustrate the problems common to all Polar expeditions (at least they were so before the introduction of aircraft) and the successful solution of those problems. In other words, this chapter will be a sort of discussion of the art of Polar exploration as illustrated by our dash to the South Pole.

Elsewhere in this volume I have described briefly our voyage to the Bay of Whales in the *Fram*. I have also sketched our winter quarters which we set up on the ice barrier, which we had reached on January 14, 1911. By the tenth of the following month, we had disembarked most of our supplies and had got far enough along with the construction of the winter quarters to permit four of us to start on the first expedition southward, to begin the essential task of establishing supply bases on the route to the Pole.

We named our winter quarters Framheim. Its location was about 78° 30' S., which means, of course, that we were approximately seven hundred nautical miles in a right line from the Pole. Our plan was to set up supply bases one degree apart (or sixty miles) as far southward toward the Pole as we could get before the autumn closed and winter made this work impossible.

Our first southward expedition comprised four men with three sledges and eighteen dogs. Each sledge carried about 550 pounds of provisions to be cached in the depots, besides the provisions and outfit for the journey. Of this 550 pounds of provisions per sledge for the depots, 350 pounds was dogs' pemmican. The other 150 pounds was provisions for human consumption, consisting chiefly of pemmican, chocolate, and biscuits. We proceeded south to latitude 80°, arriving there on February 14th. There we built our first depot. The return journey to Framheim occupied only two days, as, of course, the sledges were now practically empty.

When we returned from this first depot journey, we sat down and carefully reviewed our calculations about the remainder of our task. First of all, we now knew the lie of the ground and were thereby reassured that it was probably favourable; secondly, we knew something about the snow and ice conditions to be encountered and of the possibilities of distance to be covered per day if these conditions should be approximated on the rest of the route; thirdly, we had tried out our means of traction and had demonstrated that our theory that dogs and light sledges were the ideal combination was correct. We also had a check upon the amount of work we could expect from the dogs under heavy load conditions going south, and the extra amount of work we could expect from them under the light load conditions returning north.

We learned several other things from this journey. In the first place, it made us realize that we spent much too much time getting under way in the mornings. Two hours a day might be saved by careful planning. Secondly, I realized that our outfit was much too heavy. The sledges had been constructed with a view to the most difficult conditions of ground. We now knew, however, that the surface we should encounter was of the easiest kind and would consequently permit the use of the lightest outfit. We ought to be able to reduce the weight of the sledges by half. And, finally, our footwear needed thorough alteration. Our big canvas ski boots were too small and too stiff. They must be made larger and softer. When one is planning a march of at least fifteen hundred nautical miles over the snow and ice, he knows that lameness or foot discomfort would be a vital handicap.

This question of footwear was the subject of many earnest discussions. It led finally to our ripping apart the boots we had brought with us and remodelling them in such a way as to give them the qualities we now agreed were essential, namely, stiff soles on which our type of ski binding could be used, ample room for several pairs of stockings, soft but weatherproof ankle covering, and enough room everywhere so that the foot was not pinched at any point.

Our second depot journey was begun on February 22d. By that date, our winter quarters at Framheim were quite complete, so that on this expedition we could take more men and sledges. We left behind only one man to look after the camp and the dogs. This arrangement permitted us to make up a party of eight men, seven sledges, and forty-two dogs. On the fifth day out, we passed our depot at 80° S. and found it in good condition. Four days later we reached 81° S. We spent March 4th building and marking the second depot. Here we laid down provisions weighing 1,200 pounds. On March 5th, three of the men left us to return to Framheim. The other six of us, with four sledges, continued southward. Three days later, on March 8th, we reached 82° S. Here we established our third depot, laying down 1,350 pounds, consisting chiefly of dogs' pemmican. This was the last depot we set up. We had hoped to lay down another at 83° S., but the weather was too unfavourable; and our dogs, not yet sufficiently toughened after their long idleness on the ship, had given evidences of being unequal to the task.

As driving snow might easily obliterate these depots, we took the greatest pains to mark them for future recognition. On top of each we set up a long bamboo pole surmounted by a flag. We were not, however, content with only this precaution. Looking far ahead to the final journey to the Pole, we foresaw that in storm or fog we might easily get so far off our course as to make it difficult for us to locate a depot, even if we got into its neighbourhood. We therefore adopted the following expedient:

In the case of the first depot, at 80° S., we drew an imaginary east-and-west line through the depot and on this line set up flags on bamboo poles at intervals of approximately nine hundred yards, for a distance of about five miles on either side of the depot. This device would be an extra safeguard when we should make our way southward to the Pole or as we struggled back northward from it, protecting us in case we got off our course. Instead of one solitary marker at the depot itself, there would be drawn across our path a series of markers along a line ten miles long, close enough together so that we would almost certainly see one of them. We even marked the flags so that when we should come across one of them on the journey we would know to which side of the depot we were. This would reduce by half the time spent in finding the depot.

On our second depot journey to lay down the second and third depots, we did not have with us enough bamboo poles to mark these caches in the manner described above. What we did, therefore, was to break up some of the packing cases and use the pieces as markers. Though these pieces of wood were only two feet high, I reasoned that they were better than nothing; and considering the amount of snowfall we had observed since our arrival, they would probably be good enough.

At the third depot, we again used small pieces of packing cases which we distinguished from the others by tying to them small dark blue strips of cloth which made them easier to see. The depot itself, as usual, was marked with a flag on top of a bamboo pole.

These precautions demonstrated their value on the main journey, which began seven months later. We then encountered just such conditions of storm and fog as we had anticipated, and these markers more than once kept us from running by a depot and having to retrace our steps and waste priceless time in searching for it.

I have neglected to mention that, when we first set forth southward to establish depot number one, we marked the entire route from Framheim to the depot with bamboo poles surmounted by flags, set up at such intervals that from any one flag the next one could be perceived in the distance. We did not have enough flags to mark the entire route, and so, for the last few miles, we resorted to dried fish stuck upright in the snow! Here again, an hour or two of forethought and exertion several times saved us many hours of travel later.

After our return to Framheim from establishing depots two and three, we still had time for a last journey to depot number one before the winter set in. We utilized this opportunity to carry about a ton and a quarter of fresh seal meat to the first depot at 80° S. This enabled us on the main journey, later, to give our dogs as much seal meat as they could eat up to that point, which kept them in the best possible condition to the last possible moment.

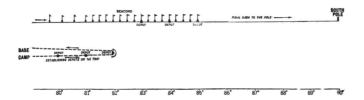

Beacons Used in the Dash to the South Pole

By the time this final journey was over, we had deposited three tons of supplies in three depots at latitudes 80°, 81°, and 82° S. The depot at 80° S. contained seal meat, dogs' pemmican, butter, chocolate, matches, paraffin, and a quantity of outfit – total weight 4,200 pounds. The depot at 81° S. contained one half ton of dogs' pemmican. The depot at 82° S. contained pemmican for both men and dogs, biscuits, milk powder, chocolate, and paraffin, and some outfit – weight 1,366 pounds.

Winter now descended upon us, compelling us to remain at Framheim until spring should follow. We were quite content, for we had done a good autumn's work. We had food supplies stored at three stations along about two hundred nautical miles of our route to the Pole. We had accumulated an invaluable fund of information about the character of the country we should have to traverse. We had determined the weaknesses in our sledges and personal equipment, and now we had the winter before us in which to alter these things so that they should be perfect when the time came for the final effort.

We set about reducing the weight of the sledge cases to a minimum. This task was allotted to Stubberud. It involved the unpacking of all the cases and their reconstruction in such form as to be equally strong, but much lighter. This was done chiefly by planing off unnecessary thicknesses of wood.

Bjaaland was assigned the most important task of all. He was to take apart and reconstruct entirely all the sledges. Our experience on the depot journeys had proved that we could save an immense amount of weight by such an alteration. Hanssen and Wisting would have the job of lashing together the different parts of the sledges as they emerged from Bjaaland's hands.

Bjaaland's workshop was a cubicle cut out of the ice of the barrier itself. It was a room about seven by fifteen feet, and six feet high. The floor was covered with shavings, and at one end stood a Primus lamp with a large tin case over it, from which steam emerged for use in softening the wood so that it could be bent. Bjaaland's task was to reduce the weight of each sledge from 165 pounds to 48 pounds, or less than one third of its original weight, without essential loss of strength. Without going into details as to the planing down of parts and the changes of design, it suffices to say that he accomplished the task triumphantly, and that his success had the greatest bearing upon our ability to reach the Pole and return.

Whenever Wisting's time was not taken up with the work of the sledges, one could hear the hum of his sewing machine. He made four three-man tents into two, and he altered our clothing to meet the conditions we had found on the depot journeys.

Every detail of these operations was the subject of repeated discussion. For example, we discussed the question of what was the most useful colour for a tent. We agreed that a dark colour was best-first, as a relief to the eyes after travelling all day on the glistening ice; second, a dark-coloured fabric absorbs more heat from the sun than a light-coloured fabric, so that on clear days on the main journey our tents would be warmer if they were dark. The tents we had brought with us were white, but one ingenious fellow suggested that we dye them with ink made from our ink powder. This suggestion seemed so practical that we soon had two dark blue tents instead of white ones. Later discussions, however, developed the probability that, after a short period of use, this dye would wash out of the fabric. The device finally adopted was to cut up our bunk curtains, which were made of a dark red cloth of light weight, and sew the parts together until we had made an outer tent to cover the one of white canvas.

Another device evolved from our discussions was a pair of stockings for each man, made of light-weight cloth. These stockings had several virtues. They not only kept out the cold of driving winds, but they also protected the other stockings against tears, so that they lasted much longer. Best of all, they proved to be easy to dry in nearly all weathers.

After these stockings had been provided for all of us, we next made a study of our underclothing. What we had brought out from home was made of extremely thick woollen material, and we feared this would be too warm. Among our medical stores we had two large rolls of fine, light flannel. Of these Wisting made underclothing for all of us. On the trip it proved to be perfect.

Dog whips were next considered. Two were made for each driver, or fourteen in all. The handles were a problem in themselves. Experience had showed us that a solid whip handle did not last long. Discussion developed the idea of a handle made of three narrow strips of hickory securely lashed together and the lashings covered with leather. This made a pliable handle that would give and bend instead of breaking.

The whip lashes were made by Hassel on the Eskimo model – round and heavy. Hansen took the handles from Stubberud and the lashes from Hassel and put them together to make the whip. All this work was done with extraordinary care. Indeed, our triple-part handle was not finally adopted until Hansen's objections to it were overcome by actual competitive trials against an alternative model designed by him, which showed that the triple handle was better. It may sound odd to the uninitiated reader that so much time and thought should be given to so simple a matter as dog whips. But the whole success of our expedition was staked upon the use of dogs as motive power, and Eskimo dogs are a hard breed to handle. They are nearly as wild and savage as wolves, and neither work nor discipline can be got out of them without vigorous use of the whip. These lashes, therefore, were almost as essential to our success as the dogs themselves.

Ski bindings next occupied us. Here every man was his own inventor, as the comfort and flexibility of the bindings is a matter of individual taste and habit. All sorts of designs were devised and tried out, and each man finally satisfied. One thing was required of all, which was that they should be easy to take off. We always had to take them off at night on the journey, for the dogs looked upon anything made of leather as a food delicacy and if one left one's bindings out for a night, they were gone in the morning. Even the toe straps had to be removed in the evening. Every detail was considered in the making of such

A small item as tent pegs. Johansen produced some that were the opposite of what such pegs usually are, being flat instead of high. This design was both lighter and stronger than the usual kind. I do not think that we broke a single one of these novel pegs on the trip.

When the clothing was served out to each man, here again everything was subjected to the test of personal experience. One man would find that the hood of his anorak came down too far over his eyes; another that it did not come down far enough; so both had to set to work at alterations – one cutting off, the other adding a piece. Everything must be suitable and comfortable before we started.

The dog harness next came in for review. The experience of our depot journeys was now utilized. On one of these trips, two dogs fell into a crevasse because the harness was faulty. We therefore devoted great care and attention to this gear and used for it all the best materials we had.

The reason for all this minute study, repeated experiment, and careful construction came out of my firm belief that the greatest factor in the success of an exploring expedition is the way in which every difficulty is foreseen and precautions taken for meeting or avoiding it. Victory awaits him who has everything in order – luck, people call it. Defeat is certain for him who has neglected to take the necessary precautions in time – this is called bad luck. The whole purpose in writing this chapter is to indicate that our success in attaining the Pole was due to the correctness of our planning. Will power is the first essential of a successful explorer – only by the mastery of his own soul can he hope to master the difficulties placed in his path by opposing nature. Both imagination and caution are equally essential – imagination to foresee the difficulties, and the caution which compels the minutest preparation to meet them.

Let me review again, therefore, the importance I attached on this South Polar expedition to our selection of dogs as motive power. We knew before we started that much of our journey would be across the great Antarctic glacier. Hidden crevasses would constantly endanger us. The selection of dogs was in part determined by this probability. If the dogs were properly harnessed together and their harness securely fastened to the sledge, the lead dog would break through the crust above a crevasse. This would give us warning in time to stop the sledge and prevent any man of the party from falling in after him. The dog himself would hang safely suspended by his harness and could be quickly dragged back to safety. Actual experience on the expedition completely justified these calculations. Scores of times one or another of us was saved from death or injury by the warning given by a falling dog.

Another advantage in using dogs requires a little explanation, if it is to be understood by the uninitiated reader. Dr Nansen, who revolutionized Arctic exploration, had brilliantly demonstrated the advantage of light equipment and the corresponding speed of movement which it made possible. The use of light sledges, of dogs for motive power, and of concentrated food for men and beasts – these were the essentials of his idea, so brilliantly demonstrated on the first *Fram* expedition. On our expedition to the South Pole, I chose dogs, not only for these reasons, but for the following additional reason:

I have described earlier in this chapter the stores of dogs' pemmican which we had carried to the three depots, and the supply of fresh seal meat we had carried to the first depot, for the dogs. I had, however, in my calculations a further idea for the rationing of these animals. I calculated before leaving Framheim exactly the weight of sledges and supplies to be carried on each day's travel southward to the Pole and northward returning. Obviously, these weights would diminish day by day as the rations on the sledges were consumed. Obviously, also, a point would be reached, from time to time, at which this weight would so far diminish that it equalled the pulling power of one dog. I made the most careful estimate of the average weight of edible flesh of a dog and its food value when eaten by the others. By these calculations, I was able to lay out a schedule of dates upon which dog after dog would be converted from motive power into food. Obviously, this scheme reduced by that much the weight of dogs' rations that had to be carried on the ledges. This reduction in weight added days to our "cruising radius" – to borrow a simile from naval language – and by that much increased our chances of reaching the Pole and returning.

This difference in fundamental planning between our expedition and Captain Scott's would of itself account for the difference in the success of the two expeditions. The gallant Scott reached the Pole, but it proved a tragic victory, for he and his men perished before they could regain their winter quarters. I had lad the gravest fears for him from the first account I had heard of his expedition, long before he left his winter quarters to make his start for the Pole. I felt sure he had chosen the wrong means of locomotion, and I gravely doubted his ability to make the round trip successfully. Scott used Shetland ponies as far southward as he could. The reader need only recall the advantage the dogs gave us in dealing with crevasses to understand the difference in the likelihood of success between Scott and ourselves.

When we made the actual dash to the Pole, we profited by another experience of our depot journeys. On those preliminary journeys, we had built a series of beacons along our line of march. They were made of snow, with a small black flag on top of each. These beacons had greatly facilitated our return to winter quarters. We decided, therefore, on the main journey, to use this method as far as possible. It proved to be not only an additional safeguard, but it also saved a great deal of time that otherwise would have been spent in taking observations and making calculations of our course. This system was especially important on the vast unbroken surface of the Antarctic continental barrier, before we came in sight of the range of Queen Maud's Mountains, whose peaks then supplied us with landmarks by which to gauge our position. As the surface of the barrier offered nothing to indicate where we were, it seemed to me only prudent to take every precaution.

We built in all 150 beacons, each about six feet high, and used in their construction 9,000 blocks cut out of the snow. In each of these beacons was deposited a paper giving its number and position and indicating the distance and direction to be taken to reach the next beacon to the north. We erected these beacons at intervals of eight or nine miles to 81 ° S. There we reduced the intervals to about five miles. These beacons, I repeat, were of the greatest value to us on our return. They reduced enormously the amount of time occupied in the mere labour of keeping on the course.

Another device was utilized to safeguard us and to save time. To each of the four sledges was attached a light wheel which carried no load, but revolved freely as the sledges advanced. Each wheel was geared to a meter which registered the number of revolutions. At the end of a day's run, a simple calculation showed the distance travelled. By averaging the records on the four wheels, we were pretty sure to get an accurate estimate. These records, of course, served the same purpose as a ship's log, and enabled us in cloudy weather to determine our geographical position very accurately when figured in connection with the course as indicated by constant compass readings.

The reader will recall that we had built three depots in the previous autumn at 80°, 81°, and 82° S. On the main journey, when we passed the southernmost of these depots, we took from it all the supplies it contained except enough to carry us back to 81 ° on the return trip. These extra supplies were to be deposited in new depots to be built as we went on south. The first of these was erected at 83° S., and contained provisions for five men and twelve dogs for four days. In the depot at 84° S, we left the same provisions, and besides, a can of paraffin holding nearly four gallons.

Soon after we established a depot at 85° S., we came to the mountains. Up to this point, we had only reached an elevation of 300 feet above the sea. We knew that now, however, we should have rapidly to ascend to elevations in the thousands of feet. To indicate the care with which we made our calculations and the mature deliberation with which we formed our judgments, I cannot do better than to quote three paragraphs from my book, *The South Pole,* written in 1912 immediately after our return to civilization:

We had now reached one of the most critical points of our journey. Our plan had now to be laid so that we might not only make the ascent as easily as possible, but also get through to the end. Our calculations had to be made carefully, and every possibility taken into account. As with every decision of importance, we discussed the matter jointly. The distance we had before us, from this spot to the Pole and back, was six hundred and eighty-three miles. Reckoning with the ascent that we saw before us, with other unforeseen obstructions, and finally with the certain factor that the strength of our dogs would be gradually reduced to a fraction of what it now was, we decided to take provisions and equipment for sixty days on the sledges, and to leave the remaining supplies – enough for thirty days – and outfit in depot. We calculated, from the experience we had had, that we ought to be able to reach this point again with twelve logs left. We now had forty-two dogs. Our plan was to take all the forty-two up to the plateau; there twenty-four of them were to be slaughtered, and the journey continued with three sledges and eighteen dogs. Of these last eighteen, it would be necessary, in our opinion, to slaughter six in order to bring the other twelve back to this point. As the number of dogs grew less, the sledges would become lighter and lighter, and when the time came for reducing their number to twelve, we should only have two sledges left. This time again our calculations came out approximately right; it was only in reckoning the number of days that we made a little mistake – we took eight days less than the time allowed. The number of dogs agreed exactly; we reached this point again with twelve.

After the question had been well discussed and each had given his opinion, we went out to get the repacking done. It was lucky the weather was so fine, otherwise this taking stock of provisions might have been a bitter piece of work. All our supplies were in such a form that we could count them instead of weighing them. Our pemmican was in rations of ½ kilogram (1 pound 1½ ounces). The chocolate was divided into small pieces, as chocolate always is, so that we knew what each piece weighed. Our milk powder was put up in bags of 10½ ounces – just enough for a meal. Our biscuits possessed the same property – they could be counted, but this was a tedious business, as they were rather small. On this occasion we had to count six thousand biscuits. Our provisions consisted only of these four kinds, and the combination turned out right enough. We did not suffer from a craving either for fat or sugar, though the want of these substances is very commonly felt on such journeys as ours. In our biscuits we had an excellent product, consisting of oatmeal, sugar, and dried milk. Sweetmeats, jam, fruit, cheese, etc., we had left behind at Framheim.

We took our reindeer-skin clothing, for which we had had no use as yet, on the sledges. We were now coming on to the high ground, and it might easily happen that it would be a good thing to have. We did not forget the temperature of 40°F. that Shackleton had experienced in 88° S., and if we met with the same, we could hold out a long while if we had the skin clothing. Otherwise, we had not very much in our bags. The only change we had with us was put on here, and the old clothes hung out to air. We reckoned that, by the time we came back, in a couple of months, they would be sufficiently aired, and we could put them on again. As far as I remember, the calculations proved correct.

At 85° 30' S. we carried out the work of slaughtering· the superfluous dogs. They provided a feast for the survivors and for ourselves. We found that dog cutlets made a delicious dinner. These were not fried, as we had neither frying pan nor butter. We found it far easier and quicker to boil them, and in this way we got excellent soup besides. Wisting, who acted as chef, put into the soup all those parts of the pemmican that contained most vegetables, so that we had the rare treat of a fresh-meat soup with vegetables in it. After the soup was devoured, we ate the cutlets. All doubts that we had entertained about the quality of the meat vanished at the first taste. It was excellent – not quite as tender as one could have wished, if an appetite had been lacking, but to us perfectly delicious. I ate five cutlets at this first meal, and would have been glad if there had been more in the pot.

At this camp we again made on paper the most careful calculations about our provisions. We went through our stock and divided it among the three sledges, as this was the point where we were to leave the fourth. The following will indicate how accurately we figured this question out. Each sledge contained:

Biscuits, 3,700 (daily ration, 40 biscuits per man).
Dogs' pemmican, 277¾ pounds (½ kilogram, or 1 pound 1½ ounces per dog per day).
Men's pemmican, 59½ pounds (350 grams, or 12.34 ounces per man per day).
Chocolate, 12¾ pounds (40 grams, or 1.4 ounces per man per day).
Milk powder, 13½ pounds (60 grams, or 2.1 ounces per man per day).

After these calculations had been made on paper, we proceeded to make the actual physical transfer of provisions. This work was done with as much care as if we were counting the gold in a bank vault. The chocolate, which by this time had broken into very small pieces, was taken out, counted, and divided among the three sledges. The same procedure was followed with the biscuits. Every single biscuit was taken out and counted, and there were several thousand of them.

Our eighteen surviving dogs were now divided into three teams of six each. We calculated that we should be able to reach the Pole from this point with these eighteen dogs, and to leave it again with sixteen.

I find the following paragraph in my record of the return journey from the South Pole:

On December 19 we killed the first dog on the homeward trip. This was Lasse, my own favourite dog. He had worn himself out completely and was no longer worth anything. He was divided into fifteen portions, as nearly equal as possible, and given to his companions. They had now learnt to set great store by fresh meat, and it is certain that the extra feeds, like this one, that took place from time to time on the way home, had no small share in the remarkably successful result. They seemed to benefit by these meals of fresh meat for several days afterward, and worked much more easily.

The next day, we killed another dog, and on Christmas Eve, another. Under date of December 28th appears the following record:

The dogs were completely changed since we had left the Pole; strange as it may sound, it is nevertheless true that they were putting on flesh day by day and getting quite fat. I believe it must have been feeding them on fresh meat and pemmican together that did this.

I shall not weary the reader with a detailed description of our success on the homeward journey. In checking our course by the beacons we had erected, it suffices to say that, time and again, they proved of indispensable aid – perhaps most specifically in enabling us quickly to find the most essential of all the depots, which was the one farthest north in the mountains. Failure to find this depot might have been fatal, for it was located at a point at which we knew we could find a safe passage down the steep descent to the surface of the barrier. Here the importance of our beacons was demonstrated with unexpected force, for, strangely enough, by reason of change in the light and our reversed direction, when we reached its vicinity the whole landscape seemed utterly strange to us. Had it not been that our beacons soon showed us the right way to the depot, we should not only have been greatly puzzled, but perhaps fatally handicapped, in our efforts to find it.

In concluding this chapter, let me emphasize again its significance. The point it is intended to make is that only the most careful planning, sound judgment, and infinite patience in working out minute details of equipment and of precaution can assure the success of an undertaking in the Arctic. These are the things that provide that invaluable "margin of safety" which is necessary to overcome the perils of unexpected difficulties and delays. Man's triumph over nature is not the victory of brute force, but is the triumph of the mind.

Footnote [1] The next thing he did was to sue me. But of course the decision went against him and he lost the suit. Then he tried the basest of all means – blackmailing. Fortunately he was stopped in this by his own lawyer. I have often wondered what changed the character of this man so completely. As a child he certainly was the most obedient and nicest of us brothers. He was "the lamb" in the family. What was it then? Inherited? Certainly not. My father and mother were the finest and most honest people in the world. Marriage? Who can tell?

Appendix

REFUTATION OF VARIOUS POINTS IN NOBILE'S
LECTURES IN AMERICA

NOTES WRITTEN BY HJ. RIISER-LARSEN, CAPTAIN
IN THE NORWEGIAN NAVY FLYING CORPS AND
THE SECOND IN COMMAND OF THE "NORGE"
EXPEDITION

Captain Amundsen has requested me as his second in
command of the *Norge* expedition, a trained airship pilot
and navigator during the polar flight, to correct the following
statements made by Mr Nobile in his lectures in U.S.A. last
autumn.

Nobile said:

"The flight from here (Vadso, Norway) to Svalbard
(Spitsbergen) I considered as one of the most difficult ones."

During this flight Nobile slept for seven hours in his
sleeping-bag, i.e. from nine in the evening till four the next
morning. We awoke him for a moment when we got a
glimpse of the Bjoroya Isle through the fog. The only thing
he did during this flight, which offered some difficulties on
account of fog and snow, was to leave the mooring mast at
Vadso and to land the ship at Kings Bay.

Nobile said:

"The Norwegians who had been sent to Svalbard had not managed to get everything in order, so I had to send up some Italians who knew these things." And he said further: "I decided to start on the 11th of May."

It was Amundsen who, after consulting the meteorologist, Malmgren, decided to leave on the 11th when Nobile the previous day had reported to Amundsen that the ship was ready for flying. Nobile did not mention that he and the Italian officer he had sent up for this purpose refused to take the ship out of the shed on account of the wind as they dared not take the risk. As Malmgren insisted that the start had to take place that day, because the good weather period was approaching an end and the coming bad weather might last long, Nobile at last consented to the manoeuvre being attempted, with the understanding that I took the full responsibility for the manoeuvre and for any damages to the ship. He said that he would have nothing whatever to do with it. He and his officer stood aside and the manoeuvre was commanded by one of the Norwegian officers, Lieutenant Hover, under my supervision.

Nobile said:

"Then came the most difficult part of the flight. I made course for Point Barrow, and gave order at which altitude to fly."

Nobile never gave one order about the course to be steered. The only thing he had to do, and did, as far as the navigation and manoeuvring are concerned, was to respond to the navigator's request to alter altitude when the latter, after consulting the meteorologist, found that we might get better weather at another altitude.

In the last part of the flight Nobile occasionally was rudderman using the elevator, but this increased the duties of the navigator, because the former was very distrait. On two occasions when the ship's bow rose a bit Nobile gave rudder to get it down again, but apparently forgot that he had done so and furthermore apparently forgot that he was at the wheel. We were just above the ice and undoubtedly would have collided with the hummocks if nobody else had watched him and taken the rudder before it was to late. On one of these occasions the stern of the ship, when this was brought gently up again, came so close to the ice that Nobile with weeping voice asked me to look aft to see if we had lost the rear engine nacelle.

With this information and the following as background one can judge of the accuracy of the statement he made in his lectures:

"On me and my work rested the responsibility whether the expedition should be carried through and whether its members ever should return."

On a third occasion when he was acting as-pilot (when he slept I was in charge of the ship) when we were ascending to get above the clouds in order to get an observation of the sun, he forgot to watch the gas-pressure. When he at last observed it, it had risen to such height that both he and we thought the envelope would burst. With a voice nearly choked by weeping he gave his orders in Italian, which happily was understood by the Norwegians. Ordinarily he spoke English.

Nobile said:

"I looked anxiously forward to the moment when we would see land, because I would have no great chances to bring the members of the expedition back to safety if we should have to land on the ice."

This is one of the very few statements in his lecture on which no correction can be brought. Nobile had no chances whatever to lead an expedition on a march over the polar ice. During the preparations he had proved that he was not able to walk even with ordinary boots on a hard snow-covered footpath without falling continuously. On account of this he claimed for himself and the other five Italian members life-insurance. If that were not arranged by the expedition they would not go with us. We had to take them, as the Italian Government made that a condition for selling the ship to us. We had to arrange it and Nobile was insured for £6000. This was so heavy an expense on the expedition that none of the others could be insured nor was insurance asked for. During our stay at Pulham a representative of the insurance company had a talk with me about this question and I assured him that in case of forced landing on the ice we should help the Italians along until we dropped down ourselves. If we should have to land somewhere on the north coast of Alaska it might happen that the non-Italians, instead of waiting several months for the fur-trading vessels, would march to Nome. Nobile was afraid to be left alone with his countrymen, not being able to march, and I had, in order to clear away that reason for anxiety, to promise him very soemnly that I should stay with them.

Nobile said:

"For the first time could I sit down in the only chair we had and take a moment's rest." [He refers to the time when we came over the coast of Alaska.]

If we add the hours he rested he probably had slept in his sleeping bag for more than six hours when we came over land on the Alaska side. From then on he slept until we had passed Cape Lisbourne, and later he slept between Serpentine River and Cape Prince of Wales, which was quite a while as we made very slow progress on account of the storm. We were then in a critical situation because the port engine was running very badly and the mechanics were too tired to respond to my order to start up the starboard engine. I am quite sure that Nobile in all slept for more than ten hours. There were not more than two or three on board who had that much sleep.

"It was I who constructed the mooring masts," said Nobile, but he forgets to say that he went to England at our expense and studied the British mooring mast constructed by Major Scott. Nobile knew nothing about mast-mooring. On his request I wrote instructions as to how the manoeuvre should be executed. I assisted him during the test manoeuvres and at his request criticized the faults that were made. Once when one of his countrymen eventually overheard my remarks he stopped me and asked me later, when we were alone, to repeat them.

In Italy we heard expressions of astonishment because we wanted Nobile with us on the expedition. The Italians said that they had several far more able airship pilots than he. In spite of this we insisted upon having him because we especially wanted the constructor of the ship with us. That Nobile was not the right pilot he proved shortly after we left Rome. He did not seem to be aware of the peculiarity of the ship, that on account of its shape it pressed downward when under speed. He became more and more nervous because the ship for a long time – until we had used a corresponding weight of fuel – seemed to be heavy, and several times he sent a rigger to the top of the ship to inspect the valves as he believed the reason to be gas leakage.

When arriving over Pulham he trimmed the ship for landing while we were going full speed, valving until she was neutral. When we approached the ground and stopped the engines in order to slow down, the ship consequently shot up through the clouds like a rocket to more than 3,000 feet altitude before we could check her. The landing here in the presence of all the British air experts is undoubtedly the greatest manoeuvre-fiasco in air-history. Nobile would not listen to the most urgent requests to trim and manoeuvre the ship in a normal way, and after several hours and many unsuccessful trials he had to ask Major Scott to assist him. The landing at Oslo was a little better but still so bad that several people whom I knew as believers in the airship as a commercial proposition lost their faith. After the landing in England some of my British friends expressed anxiety as to the fate of the expedition. At last in Leningrad, Nobile realized that the ship had to be trimmed going very slow.

Nobile tells about a storm we got into while over France but he does not say that the expedition would probably have been lost if he at that time had had his own way. We were over Rochefort, facing a heavy northeast gale with a cyclone approaching from the Bay of Biscay. We were running on two engines, making no headway whatever. Our intention had been to land in Rochefort to take on board more petrol, but landing in that gale was out of the question. I asked Nobile several times to start up the third engine so that we could make headway and thereby get away northward and away from the cyclone. Running three engines meant using more petrol per hour, but we would get to places where the wind would be weaker and we could stop the third engine again. Nobile could not understand the idea of this and refused to start up the engine until Major Scott at last succeeded in convincing him that if we ran on only two engines we would remain standing over the same spot and drift away when the cyclone came nearer, using all the petrol we had on board. Had Nobile had his way we would have probably been lost.

I think that this is enough. I am sorry that circumstances have compelled Captain Amundsen to order me to make these corrections, as I would have preferred to keep quiet.